The Search for Faith and the Witness of the Church

An exploration by
The Mission Theological Advisory Group

GS 1218

The Search for Faith and the Witness of the Church

An exploration by
The Mission Theological Advisory Group

CHURCH HOUSE PUBLISHING
Church House, Great Smith Street, London SW1P 3NZ

Church House Publishing
Church House
Great Smith Street
London SW1P 3NZ

ISBN 0 7151 5537 7

Published 1996 for the Board of Mission of the General Synod of the Church of England by Church House Publishing

© The Central Board of Finance of the Church of England 1996

All rights reserved. No part of this publication may be reproduced or stored or transmitted by any means or in any form, electronic or mechanical, including photocopying, recording, or any information storage or retrieval system without written permission which should be sought from the Copyright Manager, Central Board of Finance of the Church of England, Church House, Great Smith Street, London SW1P 3NZ.

Cover design by David Roff

Printed in England by Cromwell Press Ltd, Melksham, Wiltshire

Contents

The Mission Theological Advisory Group	vii
Preface	ix
Acknowledgements	xii
Introduction	xv

1 *Who goes there?: How people belong: some challenges to the Church*

Introduction	1
Main text	2
Summary	36
Things to do	37

2 *Pearls are for tears . . . : Challenges from implicit religion*

Introduction	45
Main text	46
Summary	67
Things to do	69

3 *The world is my oyster: How contemporary spirituality challenges the Church*

Introduction	74
Main text	75
Summary	101
Things to do	103

4 *Why world? Why oysters?: Science and the search for faith*

Introduction	110
Main text	111
Summary	142
Things to do	144

Contents

5	*From Lamb of God to dead sheep: The history of ideas*	
	Introduction	149
	Main text	150
	Summary	178
	Things to do	180

Conclusion	185
Glossary of theological terms	187
Index	189

The Mission Theological Advisory Group

The Mission Theological Advisory Group is responsible to the Board of Mission of the General Synod of the Church of England and the Churches' Commission on Mission of the Council of Churches for Britain and Ireland.

List of members

The Rt Revd Dr Michael Nazir-Ali, formerly General Secretary, Church Missionary Society, now Bishop of Rochester (Chairman)

The Revd Dr Brian Castle, Vice-Principal, and Director of Pastoral Studies, Ripon College, Cuddesdon, Oxford (from 1995)

Dr Elizabeth Harris, formerly of Westminster College, Oxford, now Secretary for Other Faiths, Methodist Conference, Methodist Central Hall, London, (from 1994)

Fr Brian Hearne CSSp, Kimmage Institute for Theological and Missionary Formation, Dublin (died 1996)

The Very Revd Robert Jeffery, Dean of Worcester, now Sub Dean of Christ Church, Oxford

The Revd Duncan McClements, Church of Scotland parish minister representing ACTS

Mr Martin Scott, Pioneer People (from 1995)

Professor Werner Ustorf, Professor of Mission, Department of Theology, Birmingham University and the Selly Oak Colleges

The Revd Alison White, Tutor in Mission Studies, Cranmer Hall, Durham

Ms Catrin Williams, Lecturer in New Testament Studies, University College of North Wales, Bangor, Dyfed, representing CYTUN

Other contributors to MTAG (1992-6)

Dr Deborah Sawyer, Lecturer in Religious Studies, Department of Religious Studies, Lancaster University (to 1993)

The Mission Theological Advisory Group

Dr Stuart Murray, Oasis Director of Church Planting and Evangelism, Spurgeon's College, South Norwood, London (to 1994)

The Rt Revd (formerly Canon) Sehon Goodridge, formerly Principal, Simon of Cyrene Institute, now Bishop of the Windward Isles (to 1994)

Staff

Dr Anne Richards, Mission Theology Secretary, Board of Mission

The Revd Donald Elliott, Secretary, Churches' Commission on Mission, Council of Churches for Britain and Ireland

The Revd Canon Philip King, General Secretary, Board of Mission

Preface

In 1992, Canon (now Bishop) John Finney published the results of a study concerning British people who had made a recent public profession of the Christian faith. This book, *Finding Faith Today*,[1] was the result of research into how people come to faith in Jesus Christ and how they journey into becoming active members of the Church. Some of the conclusions of that study were particularly interesting to those engaged in mission and evangelism. For example, it can take quite some time to become a Christian, and friends and family may have more influence over a person's decision to join the Church than the impact of the big evangelistic rallies.

Finding Faith Today, however, drew on the stories of people who had both come to faith and joined the Church. This left open a whole set of other questions. What happens to people who search for faith, who travel on their spiritual journey, who encounter the gospel of Jesus Christ and who do not join the Church? What, then, are the barriers to belief? What of people who hear the gospel and cannot or will not believe it? What of those who encounter the Christian message and respond, but balk at the idea of becoming a Church member? What of those whose faith journey leads them away from the gospel? What of those who feel that in a maze of choices, the truth they opt for cannot be the Christian truth they are offered? Are these people somehow intrinsically different from those whose stories John Finney told, or is it that they were just not lucky enough to be shown the gaps in the barrier?

We decided that these questions needed looking at with urgency and in humility. For the people who test and reject the Christian faith indict the Church particularly in terms of its ability to promote the mission of God's love to the world. There *might* be barriers which keep people out, but there might also be barriers which keep us *in*, preventing us, as Christians, from acting in mission. We had to be prepared, at the outset, to show that many barriers might be of our own making.

For this reason, we have replaced any formal introduction to our work with a letter from a fictional angry person. This letter is an amalgam of some of the views we ourselves have encountered, and which reflect on us, as

Preface

Christians, for not looking at ourselves critically enough. These views are also contained in five sections which preface the introduction to each chapter. These sections are drawn from genuine discussions with real people who commute from Essex into London.

Our response to them and to the angry letter forms the body of the work, which examines both the search for faith and the witness of the Church. We decided that we would investigate aspects of the faith journey to see where difficulties might lie, and at the same time ask if what we were learning showed that the way the Church acts in mission in the closing years of the twentieth century was contributing to these difficulties. We had to ask whether our assumptions and presuppositions about how people come to faith were outdated or lacking and whether our theology and apologetics were sufficiently developed to prevent the gospel appearing outdated or anachronistic. Our conclusion forms our own reply to the substance of the introductory letter.

In the body of the work we agreed to investigate five of the areas of modern life which in some way or other affect every person in this post-industrial, technologically oriented, and free-market-driven western society. In doing so, we resolved not to spend all our time discussing the possible ills and wrongs of our society, but to try to see how our western culture challenges us and how we might respond to that challenge. The five areas we have studied are, we think, crucial to all engaged in mission. They are: how people belong to each other and to organisations; the characteristics of implicit religion; the shapes and forms of contemporary spirituality; how science, technology and Christian faith can co-exist; and our heritage of thought and ideas.

Our methodology was to invite people working in these areas to come and challenge our thinking on these issues. Through this process we have had to look at ourselves through others' eyes and ask ourselves hard questions. A consequence of this is that we have faced these challenges together as an ecumenical group in a spirit of unity, for these challenges are common to the Christian Church as a whole. We have consulted a wide range of people, including academics, ministers, teachers, lay workers, practitioners of mission and evangelism, ordinary church-goers and non-church-goers in the process of developing this text.

Preface

For this reason, this report is also divided into sections and there are a number of different ways of reading and using it. Each chapter forms a discrete segment of the book and may be used on its own. The main text of each we hope will be of interest to pastors, teachers, academics and anyone with a professional interest. An introduction and summary of each chapter are also provided for readers who want to pick out the main points without the detail. Key words are provided for those who want to pick up on a particular area. Leaders of discussion groups or other local church gatherings may wish to use these as background material. In addition, we provide discussion starters and things to do based on the subject matter for use with church groups or other groups. We hope, therefore, that this report will not just sit on a bookshelf, but be divided up and used in a variety of ways and that the various ways of reading it will enhance each other. In particular, we hope that this report will only be the beginning of a process which allows twenty-first-century Christians to forge stronger bonds between the search for faith and the witness of the Church.

+ Michael Roffen

Note

1. John Finney, *Finding Faith Today: How Does it Happen?*, British and Foreign Bible Society, 1992.

Acknowledgements

We wish to record our gratitude for the particular contribution to this project made by Fr Brian Hearne, who died on 1 July 1996. Fr Brian brought his rich experience to the group and cared deeply about the ecumenical aspects of this work. We remember him with thanksgiving.

We wish to record our thanks to those who have assisted with this project. Our initial consultants were:

Professor James Beckford, Professor of Sociology, Warwick University

The Revd Canon Dr Edward Bailey, Network for the Study of Implicit Religion

The Revd Dr Fraser Watts, Starbridge Lecturer in Theology and Natural Science, University of Cambridge

Professor Nicholas Dent, Professor of Philosophy, University of Birmingham.

We are also indebted to comments, criticism and advice from the following:

Dr Grace Davie, The Revd Professor Robin Gill, The Revd Professor Richard Swinburne, The Revd Dr Arthur Peacocke, The Revd Dr John Polkinghorne, The Revd Dr David Wilkinson, Ms Margaret Jeffery.

The Group is also grateful to those arranging meetings and preparing the paperwork, especially Alison Ferris-Kaan and Pat Cutting.

The Group wishes particularly to record its debt to the Secretary, Dr Anne Richards, for her hard work in producing this study. Without her, this work would not even have begun, let alone come to a satisfactory conclusion.

Copyright Acknowledgements

The Group and Publisher gratefully acknowledge permission to reproduce copyright material in this book, as indicated in the list below. Every effort has been made to trace and contact copyright owners. If there are any inadvertent omissions in the acknowledgements we apologise to those concerned.

William A. Bong Ltd: Elton John, 'Blessed' (lyrics by Taupin), from *Made in England*, 1995.

Cordon Art, Baarn, Holland: *Verbum* © 1996 M.C. Escher. All rights reserved.

Acknowledgements

J. M. Dent & Sons Ltd: R.S. Thomas, 'The Other', in *Collected Poems, 1945–1990*, Phoenix edn 1995.

Faber & Faber Ltd Publishers: Sylvia Plath, 'The Moon and the Yew Tree', in *Collected Poems*, 1981; Wallace Stevens, 'The Owl in the Sarcophagus', in *Collected Poems*, 1981.

David Geffen Company: Edie Brickell and the New Bohemians, 'What I Am', 1988.

Gomer Press: Patrick Thomas, *Candle in the Darkness: Celtic Spirituality from Wales*, 1993.

The Alister Hardy Trust: Edward Robinson and Michael Jackson, *Religion and Values at Sixteen Plus*, 1987.

David Higham Associates: Elizabeth Jennings, 'Delay', in *Collected Poems*, Sinclair Stevenson, 1986.

Pink Floyd Music Publishers Ltd: 'High Hopes' (Gilmour/Samson) © 1994, from *The Division Bell*.

Oxford University Press: Craig Raine, 'Listen with Mother', in *A Martian Sends a Postcard Home*, 1979.

SPCK: The St Hilda Community, *Women Included: A Book of Services and Prayers*, 1991. Used by permission of the publishers.

Stainer & Bell Ltd: Andrew E. Pratt, 'This Web of Words and Images' © 1996. Reproduced by permission of Stainer & Bell Ltd, London, England.

A. P. Watt Ltd on behalf of Michael Yates: W. B. Yates, 'Vacillation', in *Collected Poems*, Macmillan edn 1979.

The Way, Hethrop College: J. Philip Newell, 'Spirituality, Community and an Individualist Culture', in *Teaching Spirituality, The Way*, Supplement 1995/84, Autumn 1995.

Biblical quotations have been taken from the New Revised Standard Version.

Introduction

A letter from Mrs V. Angry

Dear Mission Theological Advisory Group,

To be perfectly honest, it makes my heart sink to hear that another church body is producing yet another report on why people don't go to church. Everyone out here in the real world knows full well that the Church is years out of date. You lot don't have any clue about the kind of lives we lead, or the kind of faith we hold; you're only interested if we come in through those big heavy doors and do it your way. Yet you seem to think that if you spend a lot of time sitting round a table agreeing what our problems are, we'll all suddenly get up and start flocking into your churches – and putting money in the plate – after all, that's what it's all about, isn't it? Well, you won't find me in your cosy club – I work on Sundays!

So what good is all this advice on 'mission' going to do anyway? And just what do you mean by 'mission'? To most of us, your mission is the same as missionaries, giving Bibles to faraway tribespeople and telling them about Jesus whether they're interested or not. I suppose you'll be saying that Britain needs missionaries next! The best missionary I know is my friend, Val, next door. She may not spend every minute of her free time down the church, but she stood up for the young people when their biking area was about to be closed down. You should have heard her. She really made people think, made them look at what they were doing. I reckon Val's got a lot more in common with Jesus than the people who turned up on my doorstep the other day, asking me if I was saved and suggesting I get down to the church. They said they were evangelists. So what? My kids' tea ended up burning under the grill!

So tell me, what do these evangelists have to do with your 'mission'? And where in all this does the 'witness of the Church' come? Pretty funny witness if you don't practise what you preach: you should have seen the looks I got last time I was in church – so much for Christian love!

It's fine for you, you've got the whole story and you're so smug about it. You don't stop to put yourselves in the place of people who are struggling with questions about God, faith and religion. When I persuaded my daughter to

Introduction

see the minister about my granddaughter's christening, she came back in tears saying the kid couldn't be done without her going to church and swallowing a lot of mumbo jumbo she couldn't understand. She tried, all right, but she's miles behind. She didn't learn any of that stuff in school, you know. We're Christians too though, just not your sort. It's not fair, and it makes me angry. You write as if you've got a hot line to God and a monopoly on souls. Well, I've got my God and I'm not going to join up and toe the party line just to please you lot. Why should I? My search for faith is mine alone and I don't need some group to tell me how to go about it.

Suppose I did decide one day to go to one of your churches? Where should I go – to the place with all the singing and praying and falling about or to the smells and bells and bobbing up and down? Or should I just go to the Church of England? I see all you lot come from different churches and it's too much to hope you might have agreed on anything.

It's a pretty rotten world sometimes, but I've got my hopes and dreams and I don't see why they should all have to be taken over by your religion. And when I die, I've got my ideas about that too. Why should you always assume that I've got it all wrong? Why don't you ever shut up for a bit and find out what's really going on in people's hearts and minds?

What I want to see from a book like yours is a real attempt to listen to people like me and then to get my kind of view across to the people in your churches. Make them think about this wonderful 'witness' of yours. What's it worth to me and all the people like me? That would be a 'mission' if you like.

So, how about it?

Yours sincerely,

V. Angry (Mrs)

1
Who goes there?

My name's Jim. I've got a good job in the City. I'm well off: I have a flat and a country house I only use at weekends. At home, I have an electronic office. I send and receive by fax/modem. I surf the Net. I send e-mail. I talk to hundreds of people I've never met and would pass in the street. I'm a networker. I like having choices, like finding a new car that's just right for me. I like looking at brochures, and I belong to lots of societies and get all the glossy mags. It's good to talk and good to belong.

But as for walking into a church, forget it! All those people murmuring! All that community-singing stuff! It's years out of date. I live life in the fast lane. It doesn't fit my lifestyle. Maybe I'll want it when I'm an OAP and start thinking about dying. But I can't belong to an outfit like your Church, no way!

Introduction

In this chapter, we try to show that God's mission to people living in our society today is faced by various challenges. In particular, we look at changes: how people express their belief and how they belong to groups, networks and organisations. We seek to show further that some of the most contemporary sociological studies find our traditional thinking about community to be out of date and that people relate to each other in ways for which the Church is unprepared. Consequently, the Church may not learn to change fast enough, but may continue to promote models of believing and belonging which are no longer appropriate for those people who are searching for faith. We look into this challenge, first to investigate what sociologists are telling us and then to discover what the Church can learn. The areas which we address are particularly belonging, relationships and community. These three areas require us to look at corresponding theological areas. So when we consider belonging, we look at what the Church teaches in baptism, and at the notion of a covenant relationship with God. We have to consider what kinds of relationship are important today and how we understand what is taught to us by the doctrine of the Trinity. When we consider belonging and community, we also have to consider our ideas of fellowship, of koinonia, in terms of what it means for us to be the Body of Christ. As we do this, we try to see what this implies for mission, as we go about our task of helping people come into contact with the gospel effectively in today's world.

How people belong: some challenges to the Church

Statistics and studies

Two thirds of the nation believes in God but few go to church or believe that religion is important, according to a survey to be published next week. Most said that the various Churches were out of touch with their lives and problems and more than half said that there should be a female Pope. (*The Times*, 13 October 1995, Study for BBC Radio 2's World of Faith Week)

1.1 Radio 2 and female Popes aside, most statistical studies show that the level of 'believing' in western (including British) society remains relatively high.

British society, like the majority of west European societies, is characterised by relatively high levels of religious belief, but low levels of religious practice, a situation inaccurately described by the adjective secular. This combination of believing and belonging (a convenient shorthand) should not be taken for granted .... If belief persists, though increasingly detached from its institutional moorings, it begins inevitably to drift away from anything which might be called orthodoxy .... Indeed I would argue that this drifting of belief away from mainline Christian teaching is a considerably greater challenge to the contemporary church than the supposedly secular nature of the society in which we live.[1]

1.2 This implies that people tend to answer 'yes' to the question 'Do you believe in God?' and 'yes' to the question 'Do you pray?'[2] This shows that the majority of people have some experience of the transcendent, or have 'spiritual' experiences which lead them to understand a connection between themselves and some 'other'. More specific questions about the nature of God and God's relation to human beings lead to more diverse answers. For example:

Do you believe in a God who can change the course of events on earth?

No, just the ordinary one.[3]

1.3 This response tells us that while very basic and undeveloped forms of belief remain high, the level of support for much more specific theological ideas of traditional Christian teaching, such as the divinity of Christ, is much lower. This is an important distinction, for it suggests that the possibilities for development of a mature Christian understanding are dependent on the level of belonging to a *church*. If a developed theological viewpoint is only possible through such belonging, then this has implications for our understanding not only of contemporary spirituality (see Chapter 3), but also of the general effect on people of a decline in church-going practice. The Christian community draws its *raison d'être* from the existence of God's mission, so the churches must consider the state of the foundational worshipping Christian communities as well as the evidence for generalised external Christian belief.

1.4 The people examined in such studies may belong to any Christian denomination or none, or to another of the main religious traditions, or indeed, to a new religious movement (NRM). They may also express themselves through other forms of spirituality such as 'new age'. Despite these various backgrounds, the evidence suggests that there remains a high level of generalised Christian belief in what has been a traditionally Christian country, but which is now a plural society. This plurality also means that such generalised belief may incorporate other non-Christian religious notions, such as belief in reincarnation.

1.5 The same statistical evidence also suggests that the level of belonging to the *Church*, defined as being a practising member of a denomination of the Christian Church, is falling away from the level of generalised belief.[4] If this is true, then it indicates that people who are searching for faith, who perhaps already believe and pray to a God, do not come to locate their awakening faith within the institution of the Church, but remain outside, working it out for themselves. It should be noted, however, that some sociologists argue that there is undifferentiated decline both in believing and belonging. Others working with churchgoing data, such as Professor Robin Gill, would argue that the notion of the 'empty church' has as much to do historically with competitive building of large churches as to do with any statistical drop in numbers.[5] Also, such a decline is common to other forms of voluntary associations and is not peculiar to the Church.

1.6 Further, a tendency to immature or generalised belief may be characterised by a largely sympathetic attitude towards religious matters, and towards the Church and its institutions. For example, this general affirmation of the Church is indicated by the hurt and indignation felt by some people who have been refused baptism for their child, for whatever reason. On the other hand, in systematic pastoral visiting, it is unusual to encounter complete rejection, even if those visited would never dream of going to church. Indeed, many people wish the minister would visit them in their own homes more often. It is interesting that, given the decline in committed Christian practice, surprisingly few people have chosen not to believe, or completely to reject the Church. On the whole people do not opt for rational alternatives, but for what Grace Davie characterises as 'drifting belief'.

1.7 This implies that people do retain a strong sense of *identification* with religious life and belief but this is not matched at the level of *participation*. This emerges strongly at times of national disaster or mourning, such as at Hillsborough, or Dunblane. Conversely, it may also emerge in the maternity ward. These are times when people say what normally they keep to themselves, and often need to call on God, to express grief, or love and thanks. Paul Handley wrote in the *Independent* that the birth of his daughter made him suddenly think about mortality and death: 'her skull is so crushable: the proof of life's fragility is in my hands'. But this was not mere morbid thought, but a recognition of the importance of faith: 'Knowing, suddenly, that everybody is finite increases the desire to care for them while they are still within reach. At such a time, faith becomes more important, with at the heart of it, a murdered god.'[6]

1.8 In *The Millstone*, Margaret Drabble's character Rosamund expresses this need when her new-born baby has to have an operation:

> the subject of God did not much cross my mind, for I had never given it much thought, having been brought up a good Fabian rationalist, and notions such as the after-life and heaven seem to me crude quite literally beyond belief .... In the morning, when it was time to get up and get dressed and gather together

her pitiably small requirements, I got out of bed and got down on my knees and said, Oh God, let her survive, let her live, let her be all right, and God was created by my need perhaps.[7]

1.9   There is an assumption here, however, which must be looked at before we proceed, which is that believing somehow precedes belonging. If we look at the history of sociology, we can see that sociological thought has indicated that the relationship between believing and belonging is far from straightforward. For example, if belonging determines belief: categories of thought and feeling must originate in groups, and, indeed, there are current advocates of this idea, but there is also the notion that belief determines belonging: the model of the world that a person holds influences the group to which that person belongs.

1.10   It is important not to forget that today it is personal choices which underlie the fabric of modern society. Some American sociologists are suggesting that belonging is seen to rest with the individual's strength of commitment through choices, not collective decisions. The importance of how people see commitment in their lives today cannot be underestimated. Because the conflict between these views about believing and belonging may be unhelpful, it is perhaps better to discuss the *interaction* between believing and belonging in terms of the consequences for the mission of the Church. It is the tension between these two which will be examined in the rest of this chapter.

Figure 1   The interaction between believing and belonging

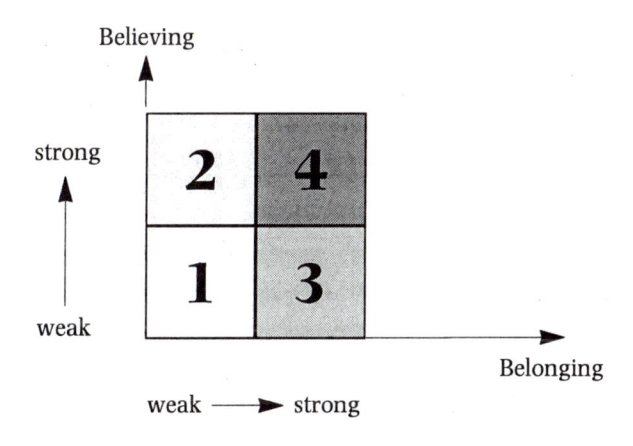

1.11 In the diagram on page 5, the strength of interaction between believing and belonging is shown by the relative darkness of the area. In number 4, the church is characterised by strong belief and commitment, a successful body, but also with rigid and closed boundaries. The mission of that church (which acts against the direction of the arrow) has to make more effort to draw itself away from the strength of its fellowship, perhaps resulting in a church plant which effectively weakens the parent church, making it look more like 2 or 3. In 1, both belief and commitment weakly interact, a struggling church, which lacks the heart of commitment to reach out to people and keep them, even if its boundaries are particularly permeable. Thus 2 and 3 may be the kinds of church which have the most mission opportunity, because the commitment (whether biased to belief or belonging) is there, but the boundaries are permeable. Such a church has the ability to reach out in mission to those outside it. Each of these kinds of situation has different mission opportunities and congregations may change their interactions in the course of their history. In considering the importance of the balance of interaction between believing and belonging, we might here be reminded of Dr Colin Morris's words: 'You cannot preach the Gospel from the strong to the weak. You can only preach the Gospel from the weak to the strong.'[8]

1.12 The type of church suggested in 3 supports Robin Gill's argument that disbelief or agnosticism is seldom a reason for lapsing from church membership or attendance. This is shown by the following illustration:

> John is in his seventies and on his own claim is an atheist, without in any way being aggressive about this. He is married to an active church member and has indicated to the parish minister that when he dies he would like the minister to take his funeral. His great joy is to be out walking on the roads and hills. He normally walks about twenty miles a day and is happiest when he is in contact with nature. Although an atheist, he helps regularly at church events, with children's outings and parties, with the disabled, and recently on a work party scraping, sanding and polishing church pews. In his bearing and attitude he is a good example of what a practising Christian might be. While he is neither a member nor a believer, he is certainly part of the fellowship at his local church.

1.13 Thus there may be many believers outside the institution of Church and many disbelievers making up the actual membership. This means that there are diffuse boundaries: the perceived understanding of the community of the faithful is not determined by the size of a congregation. Gill also argues that a conversion experience or strong recognition of belief is not always the prime reason for beginning churchgoing. People may enter casually or speculatively through the permeable boundaries of 1, 2 and 3 although they may be more likely to enter 4 after a definitive experience of being 'baptised in the Spirit' or 'born again'.

1.14 We should also remember that there are similar interactions between believing and belonging in other faith traditions in western Europe. In some faith traditions, commitment begins at home. It is clear, for example, that if a person is born into, say, an Islamic or Orthodox Jewish community in this country, that person 'belongs' to the community of that faith tradition, and will probably be expected to observe its religious practices and to marry and raise children within the tradition. In order *not* to belong to the tradition, such a person would have to 'opt out' of the belonging, and perhaps accept exile from the faith community. That person might retain a personal faith, but be unable to express that faith with the rest of the community. Often such people are required to live effectively in two worlds. It is apparent, then, that there are different interactions in relationships between believing and belonging, but what questions does this pose for the Christian churches when we look at the important points of contact: baptism, marriage, adult profession of faith, and funerals?

Christian initiation

1.15 The document *Christian Initiation and Church Membership* makes a number of important distinctions about belonging. It says:

> Belonging denotes actual, experienced participation in the life of a Christian community. It pertains to the individual's sense of identity with that community and its life of faith. It also pertains to the community's perception and recognition of the individual's involvement in its life.[9]

1.16 The document goes on to distinguish three types of belonging: informal belonging in which a person is not a recognised 'member'. Formal belonging, in which membership is legally and constitutionally understood, and belonging as 'incorporation': that is 'the union of a person with Christ and therefore and thereby with Christ's people'. Baptism, then, has a more profound aspect than merely making informal membership formal: 'an individual is thereby constituted a "person" in the community of faith as a particular church understands it'. Clearly, the interaction between believing and belonging is important here.

1.17 If we look at the practice of infant baptism, we can see that the new child is welcomed as 'belonging' to the Christian community.[10] This form of belonging, however, is related to the deeper theological significance of 'incorporation'. It is therefore a mission question how the Church helps people to understand 'belonging' in this spiritual way.

> Baptism initiates the reality of the new life given in the midst of the present world. It gives participation in the community of the Holy Spirit. It is a sign of the Kingdom of God and of the life of the world to come.[11]

1.18 The BCC document is properly concerned that, for some, baptism may appear as a static view of membership and not part of the further journey or becoming:

> Sacramental initiation marks a definitive public stage in the total process of initiation and is ordered towards a fullness of life in Christ which seeks progressively greater living actualisation, first as the initiatory process continues and then in full witness and service.[12]

1.19 This further relationship of belonging and *becoming* is therefore an important part of the mission of the Church and something which needs to be offered to people, in simple terms, at the point of contact. For example, the Church of England ASB service currently says: 'Children who are too young to profess the Christian faith are baptised on the understanding that they are brought up as Christians within the family of the Church.'[13]

1.20 Baptism, however, is also dependent on profession of the Christian faith. Therefore a public profession of faith is required *before* the admission to the community of believing Christians. So it is that an adult, or a child old enough to understand is told: 'N, when you are baptised, you become a member of a new family. God takes you for his own child, and all Christian people will be your brothers and sisters.'[14]

1.21 There is a distinction here between 'new' and 'old' modes of belonging, and new and old sets of relationships.[15] In the Roman Catholic Church this includes abjuration of Satan and 'all his empty promises' and the Church of England is considering strengthening the abjurations in its baptismal liturgy. It is suggested that there be renunciation of 'the devil and all proud rebellion against God', 'the glamour and corruption of evil', and 'the sins that separate us from God and neighbour', before the declaration 'I turn to Christ'.[16] This kind of language may suggest baptism as the fulcrum between that which is renounced, repented of and left behind and that which is entered into. This has implications for mission because mission theology describes a future into which we are all journeying which is characterised by becoming more and more like what is intended for us by God. The spiritual content of new belonging includes the adoption of a new moral order, the order of Christ's kingdom, which creates the context for God's new and final creation (*eschaton*). In this sense every baptism contributes to this forward-looking mission thinking and enhances it. Every family coming forward with a new baby therefore brings a new opportunity for proclaiming the mission of the Church. We may further extend this to say this is true of all the occasional offices.

Sacrament or passcard?

1.22 The question we have to ask here is: what is the difference between the Church's spiritual and pragmatic understanding? Do people perceive the theological significance of baptism, however dimly, or do they simply feel that baptism merely confers certain rights; in particular to call on the services of the minister for marriage in church, or for Christian burial, which was traditionally denied the unbaptised? For example: 'When Nicholas was 17, he pointed out that he wouldn't be able to have a white wedding because he hadn't been christened.'[17] The questions posed by this as a pastoral problem are debated in this example:

> [Michelle] and her fiancé plan to marry next year and ... she very much wants a church wedding. Their [incumbent], however, explained that they were not eligible, as neither of them

The Search for Faith

was baptised. 'I told him I'd be prepared to be baptised,' she said, 'but he replied that he felt that it would be for the wrong reason .... It seems so unfair that just because my mum didn't have me christened as a baby, my big day is going to be ruined.'

I ... wondered how I would have responded in her incumbent's shoes. I think I would have pursued her enquiry about baptism, which seemed genuine enough, and might have led her to a real encounter with the Christian faith. Who knows? Certainly in a country where half the babies born aren't baptised, this problem is going to become more and more common.[18]

1.23 Here, the example is based on false information. In the Church of England persons legitimately residing in a parish have the right to be married in the parish church.[19] The incumbent was wrong in what he told Michelle. However, the story has an interesting outcome:

The determined couple – apparently undeterred by their experience – had approached the vicar of a neighbouring parish. After a chat with him, they had decided to try a spot of regular church-going – with ... excellent results. 'The service was very nice,' she said, 'not at all what we expected. There were lots of couples and families and children ... and we even got a free cup of coffee afterwards.' The upshot is that they plan to make this their church, and in due course, some time next year to be married there.[20]

1.24 Here we may say that Michelle's first steps to belonging, through her desire for marriage, were resisted by the impermeable boundaries of the first church she approached, but encouraged by the more flexible boundaries of the second. In so doing, and by the particular contact of her marriage, the Church is given the opportunity to introduce her to the 'incorporation' which is spiritual analogue of her initial belonging.

1.25 What then of those who do not approach the boundaries at all? The Church finds itself challenged by those who choose to get married (if they get married at all) outside a place of worship or other religious setting. Exotic locations are particularly popular. Indeed, the *Sunday Telegraph* magazine of

7 January 1996 ran a fashion article called 'Brides on the Beach'. The implication of this article was that the perfect day includes sun, sea, a few yards of white material setting off a deep tan and the addition of the 'dream man', a seductive and skin-deep escapist fantasy which embeds marriage into an ephemeral holiday *apart* from real life. Many young people are attracted by this separation of holiday/real life, marriage/real relationship. With the changes in current legislation, marriages may now take place in hotels, country houses or other places offering a marriage 'package' and serviced by a registrar. This has implications for the opportunities open to the Church, which may for some be seen only to be competing to offer the best venue or environment for the big day. We may see a response to this in Church of Scotland practice: marriage may take place anywhere, for God is understood to be present and the Christian service is present. In this understanding, space for worship is created for the duration of the marriage service and the mission opportunity of introducing the couple to the spiritual implications of making vows before God is not compromised. What is made more difficult is the move from notional or peripheral belonging (as seen in Michelle's case) to a deeper commitment to a faith community worshipping in a particular place.

1.26 Believing and belonging, then, can come together at the point at which a public profession of Christian faith is made. In John Finney's study *Finding Faith Today*,[21] we are able to learn much from those who have made a public profession of faith, but we are required in addition to ask what happens to those who have made a similar journey towards Christian faith, but who do *not* join the Church. It is these people who also have much to teach us. Finney indicated that the average length of time it takes to find and publicly profess faith, is four years,[22] and we can learn from the ways in which the churches have adapted to the idea of extended spiritual journey, particularly in the Roman Catholic Rite of Christian Initiation of Adults (RCIA). We also have to take into account those studies of faith development which suggest that a period of not belonging, a 'sabbatical', may actually represent an important stage in faith maturity. Preliminary research based on responses by those attending the 1994 ecumenical Lent project 'Have Another Look', suggests that 41 per cent of the respondents had stopped attending church at some time for at least a year.

1.27 What happens to people who are searching for faith on their own, or who perhaps join RCIA or other Christian basics courses such as those provided by the Church Pastoral Aid Society (CPAS) or join 'Alpha' courses such as those run at Holy Trinity, Brompton, and yet do *not* end up as professed members of a particular denomination of the Christian Church?

1.28 Further, are there particular opportunities for the Church to offer genuine modes of belonging which do not fall within the usual expectations of process conversion?

Examples: some stories

In 1986, a young woman in her twenties living in Oxfordshire began to make plans for her wedding in June 1987. She read *Brides* magazine and followed its guidance for choosing dresses, flowers, cars, invitations, etc. In line with the emphasis on making the right choices for a perfect day, she visited some twelve churches of different denominations within a forty mile radius, looking at the possibilities for perfect pictures. When she found the church of her dreams, she went to the vicar and asked to fill in a banns form. When she was told that it was not possible to call her banns, she asked how she could qualify, and was told by residence, by membership of electoral roll or by Archbishop's licence. She chose to fulfil the residence requirements: the easiest minimal form of belonging. Her banns were called and she got her wish.

1.29 On the face of it, this story looks like cynical manipulation of the rules of the Church of England for individual and materialistic ends (compare David Winter's story, above). It is easy to dismiss the young woman's actions as being typically consumerist, driven by the need to make optimum choices. But we also have to ask what it was that drove her to *search* for the place in which to make one of the most important decisions of her life. What was she really looking for? The perfect setting can be created artificially if necessary. Was there a sense in which this search to belong to the 'right' place could be matched to an incipient desire to belong to the fellowship of Jesus? Are there mission opportunities in such an encounter?

A Yorkshire farmer never habitually attended church but it was traditionally understood that the local vicar would ask him to provide the stook of corn for the church at the time of

Harvest Festival. When a new incumbent was appointed, who was unaware of this tradition, the farmer was offended and upset that his traditional gift was not asked for and blamed the incumbent for this oversight.

1.30 At first glance, this seems like sheer unreasonableness on the part of the farmer, but if we look more carefully, we may see that it is all too easy to underestimate the strength of even this peripheral belonging. Here, the gift and reception of part of that person's livelihood in the symbolic form of the corn are the link to belonging, and when that belonging is undermined, a real distress may result. If we persist in seeing giving of self in terms of the body in the pew, we may overlook giving of self in ways which are none the less deeply meaningful for the giver.

1.31 A man who was an out-of-work boxer took to dropping in on the church's open morning. He was alcoholic and terminally ill with cancer and desired a reconciliation with his estranged daughter. Members of the church wrote to her, explaining the situation and finally she agreed to a meeting in a motorway café. Before this meeting the man came to church just once, arriving before the service for reassurance that he looked all right. The meeting went well and he died reconciled to his daughter. Susan Hope says of this man:

> As far as I know, Terry never made a 'profession of faith'. He never came to a church service. But he was part of us, he 'belonged'. He was 'caught' in a loving network of relationships, he participated in the life of the Body through those relationships. This is not to set up 'relationships' as the way to salvation. But this is to affirm that there are many ways of believing, some of which involve 'participation', not mental assent to credal statements. Frequently 'belonging' precedes 'believing', is a part of believing, and Pauline theology is full of a happy confusion between what it is to be 'in Christ' and what it is to be 'in the Body'.[23]

1.32 When we ponder this kind of story, we also have to remember the doubters in Jesus's time who belonged to the company, but who could not believe, and those who encountered Jesus whose lives were changed by him, but who did not enter the community which became his Church. How do those people inform our understanding of the relationship between believing

The Search for Faith

and belonging? Indeed, the sense of belonging may be very important for people where there is doubt or disillusion. It may also be important for those whose theological understanding is undeveloped (see above) and who begin at the level of trust. We may say that a missionary church will be itself a believing culture, even if it carries with it those who do not or who cannot believe.

1.33 In the diagram below, we can reconsider the interaction between believing and belonging in terms of the kinds of social, psychological and spiritual boundaries different kinds of churches create. Where there are 'soft' boundaries, there may very well be more entry points for the person searching for faith or for somewhere to belong. When we consider the people in our stories – Terry, John, Michelle, the farmer – we can see that their movement towards belonging and believing is helped by there not being a rigid barrier between the Church and the world. A 'strong' church is therefore not necessarily the most effective kind of missionary church. We shall examine later how strong churches and groups may be seen to be very successful in an age of decline, but yet not add so much to the Church's mission. In this sense they are churches of the now, prevailing against a fairly limited view of our society; they are not the churches of the future that we are challenged to become.

Figure 2 Facility of churches to be mission oriented

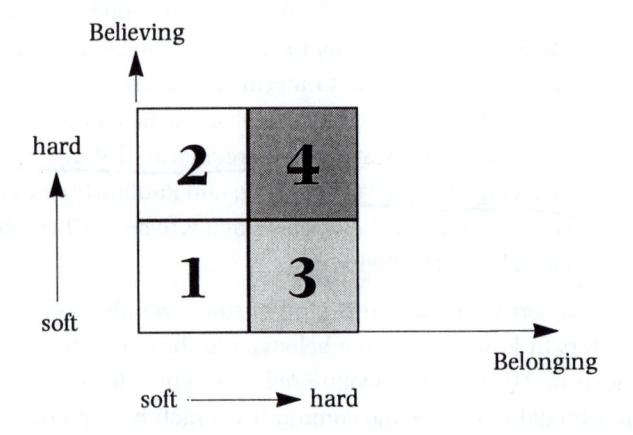

When I was at Durham I ran a very successful thing called Agnostics Anonymous for people who wanted to come along, no holds barred, no commitment, to have a drink, air their questions and their doubts, with no prayer, nothing religious at all, it was just a general free-for-all. It was highly successful: it never surprised me when people started to drift into the church and sit at the back and come and go. And what I *long* to see is a Church that is *open* to the community, so that people feel they *can* come on their own terms, and move away on their own terms too. That's how the Church ought to be.[24]

1.34 If we look at such stories in detail, it is possible to see that the relationship between believing and belonging is extremely complex. Believing and belonging are not only related, but form part of the same sociological, anthropological and theological processes.

Scriptural models

1.35 We also have to take into account the idea that Christian belief may actually be *about* belonging. First, we cannot underestimate the biblical sense that people are created in the image of God (cf. Genesis 1.26) and thereby 'belong' to the Godhead. We can see this reflected particularly in the use of the personal pronoun. God speaks of 'my people' (e.g. Exodus 3.7; Leviticus 26.12; Jeremiah 12.16), Jesus says, 'Feed my lambs' (John 21.16). There is also a strong sense of 'keeping' and 'entrustment' between the Son and the Father, so Jesus says to God, 'I did not lose a single one of those whom you gave me' (John 18.9). Part of the nature of God is the ability to keep, or to remember all human beings (cf. Genesis 8.1; Exodus 6.5; Psalm 105.8,42), so that, in an ancient image, those who sail in the ship of God's saving promises *cannot* be lost in the storms and rough seas of the world's troubles.

1.36 This important sense of belonging is made concrete in the idea of a covenant between God and human beings as in the case of the covenant with Noah (Genesis 9.8–17); with Abraham (Genesis chapters 15,17); the covenant with Israel on Mount Sinai (Exodus chapters 19,24); and with David (Psalm 89; Jeremiah 33.19–26). The idea of covenant is a powerful purveyor of confidence, community, purpose, promise and integrity. Where covenant breaks down there is bewilderment, scattering, self-examination and lament. We can see this in Deuteronomy 29.24–25: 'they and indeed all the nations will wonder, "Why has the Lord done thus to this land? What caused this great display of anger?" They will conclude, "It is because they abandoned the covenant of the Lord."' (Cf. Psalm 78.37; Jeremiah 22.8–9; Zechariah 11.7–11.) In the Old Testament, the act of making a covenant confirms the sense of belonging, so that the Ark of the Covenant becomes a visual holy symbol of the mutual promise of belonging between God and his people (e.g. Exodus 25.10–22; Deuteronomy 10.1–11; 2 Samuel 6.1; 1 Kings 8.1–9), and circumcision becomes a symbol of belonging to the covenant. Genesis 17.11 says: 'You shall circumcise the flesh of your foreskins, and it shall be a sign of the covenant between me and you' (cf. Acts 7.8). Further, the covenant is exclusive: other tribes and clans cannot 'belong' to God in this way, and are marked out as 'other'. Even more important, the covenant is guaranteed and underwritten by other forms of belonging, in particular the governance of, or access to, land (cf. Genesis 12.1–3; 13.14–17; 28.13–15), 'a land flowing with milk and honey' in Deuteronomy 6.3; 11.9; 26.9, so that the Babylonian captivity and the Diaspora generate a terrible sense of dispossession and exile (e.g. Amos 7.17; Jeremiah 4.5ff.; 6.1ff.). While it is clear, as will be shown, that the idea of territoriality is no longer always appropriate in models of belonging, we should not perhaps ignore the psychological satisfactions of the covenant relationship. Further, an examination of the sense of being lost and the need for restoration might well provide the churches with information about how to reach those who search for faith but do not join the institution of the Church, or indeed any other religious institution.

1.37 When we consider the theological model of God's covenant with all of humanity and, indeed, with all creation, we have to ask how this relates to the New Covenant instituted by Jesus as well as to the kinds of covenants which some churches (and new religious movements) ask their members to enter into. In all of this, there is the question of criteria for belonging within or under the covenant. Who decides who belongs and who does not? If God is by nature inclusive, loving and merciful, what criteria exist for refusal?

1.38 This feeling is often expressed by people whose request for baptism of their child is refused, except on the 'condition' of attending church and/or receiving instruction. In particular, some people may feel that their new child is being rejected as 'not good enough', or that their lifestyle is being criticised and used as a disqualification for their child. They may therefore see the idea of receiving instruction, not as help but as a trial. We may see such feelings as indicating the bewilderment some people experience when the Church attempts to 'rush' them from undeveloped to developed theological view through the entry point provided by the baptism request. The idea of the spiritual journey through which the love they experience for their new child is deepened and explored as the child grows may be the least complex entry point for many people encountering theological ideas for the first time.

1.39 Here, it might also help to remember that in the New Testament, Jesus calls the disciples into a fellowship which is not immediately contingent on exactly what or how they believe. It is worth noting that according to Mark 6.52 the disciples are utterly astonished when Jesus walks upon the sea 'for they did not understand about the loaves, but their hearts were hardened' (cf. also Mark 4.13, 40; 8.17–21). Moreover, John stresses that it is only after the resurrection that the disciples will fully understand (cf. John 12.16; 14.29). Indeed, the sense of belonging with Jesus is not undermined by their lack of faith or lack of understanding. As the sense of belonging is strengthened, so understanding grows until the disciples and Peter can acknowledge that the Rabbi, Master, Teacher is also friend and Lord and, indeed, the Christ (cf. John 6.69; Mark 8.27–30). Yet this same Peter, on whose rock the Church is founded (Matthew 16.18), is also the Peter who denied any sense of belonging with, or to, Christ (cf. Matthew 26.69–75; Mark 14.66–72; Luke 22.56–62; John 18.15–18, 25–27). According to the fourth Gospel, Peter's threefold denial of Jesus subsequently parallels his threefold confession of love for Jesus (John 21.15–19). The paradox of these pictures of Peter in the gospels may help us in forming an approach to how people believe and belong today.[25]

1.40 The fellowship of the disciples with Jesus may be said to create the conditions under which the faith of the early Church is fostered. Under these circumstances, believing as a wholehearted commitment is conditional upon belonging as a nominal commitment. Obedience to the command to 'follow me' (e.g. Matthew 8.22; 9.9, 19–21; Mark 1.17; Luke 18.22; John 21.19) represents only one step on a continuing journey.

1.41 For these reasons, this chapter now looks at a number of different kinds of belonging which are current in modern society and considers the levels of commitment which may be associated with them.

Belonging to me

1.42 The most basic form of believing and belonging concerns the establishment of identity. 'What-ness', 'Who-ness' and 'Where-ness' are all necessary to a person who needs to make sense of being alive. The ability to state one's name and location is the first investigation in any neurological examination. However, some neurologists and psychologists also see the ability to establish identity as a prerequisite for spirituality and religious awareness. The neurologist Dr Oliver Sacks speaks of a profoundly amnesiac man as being 'de-souled' because the lack of memories of himself could not allow him to 'belong' to the present. Yet this man is entirely transformed at the eucharist:

> I saw here an intensity and steadiness of attention and concentration that I had never seen before in him or conceived him capable of. I watched him kneel and take the Sacrament on his tongue, and could not doubt the fullness and totality of Communion, the perfect alignment of his spirit with the spirit of the Mass. Fully, intensely, quietly, in the quietude of absolute concentration and attention he entered and partook of the Holy Communion. He was wholly held, absorbed, by a feeling. There was no forgetting, no Korsakov's then, nor did it seem possible or imaginable that there should be; for he was no longer at the mercy of a faulty and fallible mechanism – that of meaningless sequences and memory traces – but was absorbed in an act, an act of his whole being, which carried feeling and meaning in an organic continuity and unity, a continuity and unity so seamless it could not permit any break.[26]

1.43 We should also remember that when Jesus healed the man whose name was 'Legion', his healing was signalled by the recovery of identity, selfhood and religious awareness: he was 'clothed and in his right mind' (Luke 8.35).

1.44 This important sense of belonging to oneself gives a person the ability and authority to talk about 'I', and also to understand that no one else can be 'I'. Following Buber,[27] we can say that this in turn creates the conditions for relationship, for bonds and bridges to be established across boundaries to 'thou' (other human beings) and 'Thou' (God). This means that the giving of names is extremely important and so is location. We may see this exemplified in the status of the creation stories in Genesis (e.g. 1.5,8,10). We can also see this reflected in biblical examples of God calling individuals by name, such as in the call of Samuel (1 Samuel 3) and of Paul (Acts 9.4; 22.7; 26.14), and by encounters with God in sacred places, such as holy mountains (e.g. Exodus 3.1–6). The most primitive kind of belonging, then, is the establishment of an I–Thou relationship.

Individualisation

1.45 Today, however, we have to take into account new sociological processes. Together with the establishment of identity, it is also necessary to see the process of individualisation as being significant for believing and belonging. 'Individualism and secularisation are behaving like a pair of scissors, each of the two blades contributing to a situation in which moral choices are becoming individual choices.' This also means that 'Individualisation makes religious people more critical of the institutionalised aspects of religion and de-institutionalisation of religion will, in the long run, lead to a loss of religiosity.'[28]

1.46 In today's society, then, the sense of self is sharpened by the process of individualisation to a point where individual experience and understanding are placed over against tradition and teaching. This is what is meant by 'individualisation'. It is important to understand that this is a critical stance which necessarily weakens belonging in terms of 'solidarity' with others, although the need to *rely* on others may actually become stronger. It is not actually possible to 'live my own life' without a high degree of dependence on what other people can provide. We will see in the contemporary spirituality chapter that New Age, alternative therapies and new social movements seem to appeal mainly to the most individualised people today. This means that the first assertion of the self may be that 'I am myself and I do not belong to anyone'. Alternatively, this may be extended into a monistic sense that the self is (or can become) God. These views may also imply that such a person will also reject the Church where the Church is seen to wish to have a directive or dominating influence. The artist Stanley Spencer, for example, talked about the power of his individual artistic vision as 'the Church of me'.[29] For many people today who are nominally Christian, spiritual experience may be reduced to 'the Church of me'. However, as with Stanley Spencer, the 'Church of me' may contain rich and valuable insights into spirituality. What is the Church going to do about this? How can it use these insights?

1.47 Set against this, we have to consider how people behave in solitary confinement. For some people, such as those in prison, this is used as punishment. The deprivation of stimuli from others causes the sense of self to disintegrate. For example: 'My thoughts were frequently occupied by the loss of my humanity. What had I become? I walked the floor day after day, losing all sense of the man I had been, in half-trances recognizing nothing of myself.'[30] In other cases, such as hermits and solitaries, the isolation of self strengthens the power of the bond with God, but this is still dependent on the support of others in relationship:

> Even Christian hermits, if they are to flourish, need not only the prayers of the community but also to be in some form of continuing relationship. If we take seriously our baptism as making us fellow members of the body of Christ, then it is not something to be pursued alone, but something to be received through mutual ministry, encouragement, fellowship and love.[31]

1.48 This raises the question of distinction between 'individual' and 'person', especially if we remember the point about baptism conferring personhood within the Body of Christ. Part of the process of 'individualisation' is the notion that people can in fact exist as individuals, without considering what is implied by personhood. In solitary confinement, the individual may survive, but the *person* may be severely affected by being deprived of relationship.

1.49 This poses a problem for the Church where the sense of self is measured against what we understand by 'God'. The 'I–Thou' opposition has a relational value, but some theologians, such as Alistair McFadyen, also see the sense of personhood being created, or 'sedimented', through the aggregation of interpersonal relationships. In this case, the 'Thou' which is God is specifically the Triune God and this understanding of personhood in relationships is derived analogously from the theology of Trinity.[32] There is a problem here, however, when we consider the existence of autistic people, who are unable to endure social contact or form relationships in the way we understand them.[33] A woman whose story is recounted in another of Dr Oliver Sacks's books gives her ontological perception to the title: she feels herself to be 'an anthropologist on Mars'.[34] None the less we may find it revealing that this lady, who from an early age was unable to bear her mother's touch, later built herself a machine, which, under her control, could simulate holding and cuddling her. Similarly, although she only believed in an impersonal or 'scientific' God, she was able to react intuitively to animals and to their behaviour.

1.50 From this, we may have to have a theology of mission that says we must recognise a fundamental self, which stands over against the personhood of sedimented relations. This fundamental self is both ontological and eschatological; it is part of our being when we come into existence and as we die. Further, this fundamental self has an urge to relationship; its existential condition is relational. The notion of belonging, then, is rooted in this urge to form relationships. Where people are unable to make inter-personal relationships, or where their lifestyle impedes this, we can infer that their notions of believing in a personal God and their notions of belonging, as to a Christian community, will be impaired. This kind of understanding will be developed, as it becomes crucial, in a later chapter.

1.51 It is clear that some of the processes of individualisation may well work against the idea of the person made in the image of a Triune God, and lead to the formation of a God-sense which is in fact antithetical to some understandings of Trinity. It is also not enough to proclaim the missionary God as one who is Father, Son and Holy Spirit, without first creating contexts for people to receive this idea.[35] We can also see that the interaction between believing and belonging may be related to the sense of 'who I am'.

Post-materialism

1.52 Another question which arises from the process of individualisation, is whether post-materialism, the emphasis on quality of life, tends to bring with it the idea that the individual will *always* be able to make choices in order to define 'who I am'. This affects even the most basic kinds of belonging, so that, for example, the Children Act now intends to put the interests of children and their wishes at a premium, meaning that under certain circumstances, children can 'divorce' their parents. There are more choices about belonging than ever before, and the emphasis on quality of life in a 'pick'n'mix'[36] society means that many opportunities for this arise in response to consumer demand. We can see this in the High Street, where there is a large range of, say, fast food restaurants, which all essentially offer the *same thing*. We can also see this in the different practices and therapies which constitute New Age.

Belonging to the family

1.53   The second important process of belonging is the formation of closely bonded relationships with other human beings to become members of a family. Underlying this, we have to recognise that the most important factor in human bonding is sexuality. Also, we may see reproduction and nurture as the historic basis of natural ordering. The Jewish *Kaddish* reminds us that 'with our lives we give life. Something of us can never die.' The sharing of name (and sharing of genes) fosters powerful bonds of association which in many societies extend out into clans and tribes. Traditionally, families were also closely located in a geographical area.

1.54   We may notice also the emphasis religions have put on the importance of the family, from the Christian example of the Holy Family to Orthodox Jewish insistence on the holiness of the family. While there may be segregation of the sexes in the synagogue, the mosque, or in churches, prayers and ritual actions at meals in the home may have a powerful bonding effect. The family is reminded that it belongs to each other and to God. We may also note that hospitality is closely related to embassy and is itself a part of mission. Jesus himself instituted the Eucharist in the Jewish Passover tradition, but even practising Christian families do not necessarily make their meal times referential of God. Indeed, in an age of TV dinners and microwaved snacks, the communal meal is impractical for many. None the less, the fact is often overlooked that the family represents a powerful missiological force, in the simple terms of handing down the message of faith to other generations. Here, we may consider the considerable importance of those grandmothers in the eastern bloc who nurtured the faith in private and passed on the Christian message to their grandchildren, keeping the faith of the community alive while religious practice was suppressed by the authorities.

1.55 It is also important to mention the significant role that women have traditionally had to play in this process. Even in times when the notion of family is changing, women, as the bearers of children, cannot be overlooked as the major influences in the religious lives of those closest to them. In *Finding Faith Today*, the biggest influence on men in finding faith was the influence of the spouse.[37] Here we may be wise to consider the openings provided by human relationships, especially those between women and men and women and children, where the experience of being loved provides openings for the Church to proclaim God's mission of love to the world.

1.56 The gender question is important, for it may be that women are in many roles able to talk about love and relationships more freely than men. The evangelisation of some men therefore also involves giving them an appropriate vocabulary and the permission to use it. Without this, the situation of some is seen to be tragic. Martin Robinson writes about some groups of working-class men for whom:

> Just occasionally there seems to emerge the sense that there might be something more than the merely physical. It is almost as if the existential encounter of people with the world occasionally suggests a religious dimension, but a knowledge of how to express such feelings is absent. In any case, it is as if the emergence of such feelings must at all costs be denied and suppressed, kept so firmly within the realm of the private that such longings dare not be admitted even to those few people with whom one shares some intimacy – one's friends, one's lover, one's wife.

The picture that emerges is of people who are truly lost.[38]

1.57 The importance of relationship breaking down these barriers of silence and lostness is, as has been shown above, incorporated in the baptism service, but it is also offered by some new religious movements in which a person is incorporated into a new family of loving relationships and separated from their original family where that family is outside the movement. Where this happens, belief and belonging are required to be synonymous and the adherent is required to make a choice for this, often to the great distress of the abandoned parents, brothers and sisters, husbands, wives or children.

1.58 However, we must now acknowledge that the nuclear family and its relationship networks are no longer the only appropriate model of 'family' in existence in western society.[39] Belonging is complicated by a greater number of relationship possibilities and by greater geographical distances between parts of the kinship network.[40]

1.59 For example, Canon Peter Challen, formerly of South London Industrial Mission (SLIM) found it necessary to use in his own work the following definition of the family to describe its mode of belonging:

> A family is a unit which endeavours to be stable, loving and caring; within which the value of each individual and entity is recognised and where the interaction of each member and each part builds and nurtures enhancing relationships and a developing and accepting interdependence.

1.60 He points out that this could include other family-like structures, for instance: the earth itself; the whole of humanity; a nation; a corporate team; a unit without blood ties; a local community; a tribe; a conventional or unconventional blood affinity; a legally registered family. This raises questions about where the boundaries between various groupings may lie, especially where these may be unclear but undoubtedly operational. Consequently, there is some caution to be exercised in talking about the 'church family' and its members, for the church community may or may not have the characteristics of a family. Sometimes where the term is used, it unhelpfully appears to exclude the contribution of single people.[41] At the same time, the Church may properly have an important opportunity to be community or family to those with no family. The problem seems to arise when the Church formulates a model of family which is then forced on people, rather than encouraging people to find family-like networks which may better suit their needs. These might include youth groups, or mother and toddler groups, for example.

1.61 The process of individualisation may also give the individual more sense of choice in defining 'who is my family?' It is interesting in this respect that Jesus himself asks the question 'who is my family?' in relation to belonging. Not only does he ask this question directly in Matthew 12.48, but he also asserts his sense of belonging in the Temple, as over against the assumed bonds to his parents (Luke 2.48–49), and restores the sense of familial belonging, broken by his death, by giving the care of his mother to the beloved disciple (John 19.26–27). In this way, Jesus has something to say about priorities in belonging which point to right relationship between human beings and God.

Belonging to a community

1.62 In larger groupings we must differentiate between familial belonging and that of community. Traditionally, the idea of community was geographical or territorial: the immediate neighbourhood and the families living within it were most important to the notion of belonging: 'I am x and I come from y ....' Consequently, in some places, a communal model of religious life is most usually apparent. Everyone in the community sees the village church as 'their' church irrespective of their actual membership. This model, therefore, has particular ecumenical implications.

1.63 Further, in inner-city and developed areas, neighbourhoods may be much more difficult to define, except in ghettos and housing estates. Consequently, community groupings may occur on the basis of ethnic origin or through other networks, requiring churches which fulfil the function of responding to the conditions of entry. This vision of the Church which sees a movement from territory to network has been addressed in the context of church planting: 'many ... are asking for recognition that human life is lived in a complex array of networks and that the neighbourhoods where people reside may hold only a very minor loyalty.'[42] This means that the Church must re-examine the whole notion of 'community'. For example, the Basic Christian Communities of Latin America, Africa, and Asia, together with the New Churches may show the Church how different kinds of community can nurture the faith in ways appropriate to particular contexts. The idea of 'community' as a dense, positively charged concept may in fact be unhelpful today,[43] and where this is so, we can see that it may well be the task of the Church to put people in touch with appropriate networks.

1.64 Another way in which the individual's sense of belonging is changing is in location and orientation. In today's western culture, the majority of people make use of transport and are familiar with planes, cars and ships enabling them to travel large distances in a relatively short time. This increased mobility blurs traditional ideas about 'belonging' to a particular place in common with all the other people who 'belong' there. A person may simply have a set of 'landmarks' which constitutes his or her belonging. These might include a house, an office, a leisure centre or club, and perhaps a church, all at some distance from one another. The different people encountered at each of these 'landmarks' might only have that one person in common. How, then, does the Church equip Christian people and those searching for Christian faith to see the church as the centre of their network of locations and to relate their spirituality to all these other landmarks? This is a significant mission question. For example, if you live in Southampton but work in London, how do you invite your colleague who is searching for faith, but who lives in Birmingham, to come to church with you? When John Finney has shown the importance of *relationship* in making faith commitments, this kind of question becomes acute.

1.65 There is also another important question about what role religion has to play in institutional life. The way that religious issues are reported or portrayed in the media, the way that religious festivals are respected (or not), the way public ceremonies include religious rituals, it might be that all this can come to represent the common religious denominator between the various aspects of a person's life.

Belonging in contemporary society

(I) CHOICE AND PARTICIPATION

1.66 The process of individualisation and the use of networks also mean that a person is exposed to possibilities of belonging which are not predetermined but offered as choices in the course of that person's lifetime. Contemporary society offers the possibility of choosing friends, one's marriage partner, and a whole series of societies, groups and networks which are representative of allegiances, interests and beliefs. The local social system is usually seen to be made up of overlapping networks, primarily those relating to education, leisure, kinship, politics, and trades union or other groups.

These create a 'network infrastructure' which have nodal points where they 'stack' or 'overlap'. Such networks may also be directly related to the important geographical landmarks, so where 'school' is one such landmark, the associated networks may include after-school activities or Parent Teacher Association. The identification of these nodal points may in fact be crucial for discovering where and at what times an individual may become susceptible to interest in joining a church. It is a challenge to the Church to have the notion put before it that individuals become receptive to outreach in mission through these networks. It is an indictment of the Church's activity, however, that receptive groups may be seen as the merely vulnerable by others. 'To target the vulnerable' is manifestly not the same as 'evangelising the receptive'. Here, then, we have to draw attention to the need in the Church to develop sensitivity in evangelism, and to draw a distinction between what is appropriate evangelistic activity within receptive groups and unacceptable proselytism.

1.67 The New Churches, for example, are good at using networks to gain access to people in receptive groups, such as young parents on housing estates. This form of approach is also, in fact, implied in *Breaking New Ground*, where a church plant of a particular type may be the most appropriate mission strategy in an underchurched housing estate.

1.68 We can also see this operating in very specialised areas. Some new religious movements are able to 'target' young people in institutions of Higher Education very successfully. Others, whose primary strategy involves 'walking the walk and talking the talk' are very effective at mobilising the network of friends at work in order to attract possible converts.

1.69 Joining networks, however, presupposes the exercise of membership, of participation. Being a supporter of a football team or of a pop star's fan club also presupposes the desire to attend football matches or pop concerts. Doing so strengthens loyalty and the bond of relationship not only with what is believed in (the club, or band) but with those others who share the common interest. But this phenomenon of the strong core group, with its powerful bond-making, is also declining in favour of the central interest being mediated through television, magazines, and other forms of marketing.

The Search for Faith

(II) CHOICE AND NON-PARTICIPATION

1.70 One of the most significant shifts in contemporary society is that of non-participatory belonging. That is to say, feelings of solidarity with the chosen society or group are reinforced not by contact or relationship with other human beings, but by other media. Therefore many people think it is perfectly possible to be a Christian by watching *Songs of Praise* and singing along with the hymns and may derive great pleasure from doing so. This phenomenon is also signalled by the rise in membership of correspondence organisations, from which people receive information and special items in their homes without direct participatory requirement. Typically, there is a core group of deeply committed and active members and a much larger group of non-participating members who simply read about the activities of the core group. Commitment is reflected only at the level of financial investment.

1.71 This loss of interactive behaviour is also present in other parts of life, such as mail-order shopping, banking by phone, and passing mail on the Internet, indicating feelings and emotions by little symbols (:-) (:-((turn this page sideways). Quick, convenient, impersonal processes eat into traditional relationships with threatened loss of shared experience and oral tradition – something which advertising and television tend to exploit ('Get through to someone' and 'It's good to talk' are the slogans attached to BT advertisements). The mobile telephone promises instant access without the necessity for face-to-face encounter. Some tabloid newspapers exploit the lives of characters in soap operas, replacing actual community news with a focus on the common fiction beamed three or four times a week to every household. This represents a satisfaction with belonging at one remove, a peripheralising and isolation of individuals in the name of their own choices or convenience. Faith and belief are therefore isolated and less likely to be shaped or challenged in the common arena.

1.72 Consequently, if for many people life is no longer lived in intense face-to-face personal relationships, then the Church may have to ask itself whether the kind of worship it offers can accommodate such people. How does the Church provide for those who desire a distant, formal and self-protecting way of relating? Perhaps this means that those who attend a quiet service at 8.00 a.m. on a Sunday morning should be seen as Christians whose church life mirrors their world life. Perhaps they do not experience a split between their religious life and daily life, whereas those who participate in intense affectual worship on a Sunday may find this untransmissible in the rest of their networks and relationships. The Church might well have a need to allow people to relate in non-intense ways.

Belonging to closed societies

(I) BOUNDARIES AND COMMUNITY

1.73 If we look at religious groupings, we can see that a proportion of these have reacted by becoming increasingly closed. Hard and fast boundaries tend to form between the community of 'us' and those who are 'other', a phenomenon which has had repercussions in other areas, particularly with regard to racism. One example of a closed society is the Christian sect known as the Exclusive Brethren which regards the world as intrinsically corrupt and its inhabitants as therefore potentially contaminating. This means that Exclusive Brethren prefer not to take part in public or democratic processes and lay their emphasis on self-examination. Needless to say, for some exclusive communities the price is extinction, since losses due to deaths and expulsions are not replaced in increasingly ageing communities.

1.74 Some new religious movements also develop similarly rigid boundaries, leading to the development of beliefs and practices designed to prevent loss of membership. Such practices include the maintenance of devoted allegiance, the taking away of possessions from 'outside' the group, or insisting that leaving the society will result in damnation, judgement or retribution. Being a member of such a closed society sometimes requires that members belong to no other form of network or grouping, even sometimes family groupings. This conditional belonging is thus concentrated in the closed society, and can be very attractive to people who find the kind of belonging offered by other areas of their life unsatisfactory. In particular, the strength of the new convert's adherence may shear against family notions of belonging and cause much distress to those left on the outside, who are conscious that their notions of the way the convert 'belongs' to them have been irreparably damaged. There is also a split in perception between 'inside' and 'outside', where parents and friends see the religious groups as possessive and manipulative, but the person on the inside may experience security, peace and freedom from other responsibilities and anxieties, and intense caring and love.

1.75 We may see echoes of this in certain sections of the mainstream religions. A groundwork of belief in a set of basic truths makes for closeness and a deep sense of spiritual oneness. This closeness may be registered in the powerful community ties of fundamentalist Muslim factions, in the insistence of the absolute authority of the Pentateuch by some Hasidic and other Orthodox Jews or in the ecstatic worship of some charismatic congregations. This closeness may none the less be felt as threatening by other communities who feel there is no room for dialogue when belief and belonging are so powerfully integrated. Some such closed communities may also use their feelings of strength and confidence in their hard boundaries in a missionary outreach that is not by witness and example but by engulfment: a mission imperative to see what is 'other' become 'self'. This makes sensitivity in evangelism difficult to maintain, and 'targeting the vulnerable' may be the result. This is not a religious perspective to be set alongside others, but a response to an instinctive and overriding 'rightness' that necessitates the condition of belonging. These high-definition *religious* groups are often fast-growing in highly secularised societies.

1.76 In this section, we must also consider the traditional role of religious communities. Here, the mode of belonging can be understood as producing a situation where each individual is community. In closed orders, particularly, all the networks of a person's life are subsumed within the location of the community house and gathered into the life of prayer. In the sociological terms we have been discussing, the religious community becomes a focal 'nodal point'. We may also say that such a mode of belonging challenges much in modern life. We also have to distinguish between different kinds of religious community, particularly those whose members work in the world and the contemplative orders. These too may be changing:

> Curiously, the new forms of Christian community which are developing are often ecumenical, for example L'Arche and Taizé. Just at the point that the great institutions of the religious life in the Catholic Church are declining, the concept of radical Christian community is spreading into other denominations and being radically reworked. As part of this new

development, there are expanding possibilities for lay ministry, and new forms of Christian community which are often ecumenical and mixed gender.[44]

1.77   There are other communities living under a rule of common life, such as that at Iona. All of these provide models of how commonality of belief and belonging can focus the witnessing potential of that community in an enriching way. Sr Lavinia Byrne writes that by giving everything up, she has been given back everything. 'Sometimes I've scurried around looking for the treasure in the religious life, whereas the treasure was the transaction. I sold everything. I gave away everything. And now everything belongs to me. Everything.'[45]

(II)   AT WORK

1.78   Interestingly, this close correlation between believing and belonging may also be seen operating in some work environments. Some companies are analogous to those certain NRMs which keep members by tacit threat, maintaining absolute allegiance (even where it means breaking the law) by the constant concern for keeping their jobs (unemployment as damnation and punishment). Other companies use the relationship between believing and belonging as a market strategy. For example, the Body Shop sells its products through promoting belief in concern for the environment, being against cruelty to animals and articulating Anita Roddick's view that natural products can enhance human wholeness and lifestyle. It is important, then, that the staff who 'interface' between products and public, are seen to endorse these beliefs (for example, through wearing T-shirts) and to stand for caring ecology. The 'right' person for Body Shop jobs is therefore one with the proper attitude and willingness to believe the message which is being given to the public. This is to make selling into a kind of missionary activity.

Belonging to Christian denominations and the Church of England

1.79   In *Last Seen Wearing*, an episode of the TV drama series *Inspector Morse*, Morse asks his sergeant, 'Lewis, are you a Catholic?' Lewis looks puzzled. 'No sir, just the usual.' In other words, as any hospital receptionist well knows, the default denomination in England is the C of E. There is the feeling that the established Church, being 'of England', is allied to nationality where that is English. This also means that the Church of England is more likely to have more modes of open belonging than closed committed belonging. Roman Catholics who no longer attend church are more likely to describe themselves as 'lapsed', i.e. out of a particular kind of belonging, than Anglicans who may make little distinction between attendance and non-attendance in terms of belonging. However, this further means that where Anglican congregations have changed from an open model to a 'gathered' model, based on identified membership, other denominations and marginal Anglicans have found themselves suddenly disenfranchised of the nominal belonging which may actually have been important to them.

1.80 Grace Davie has also identified a trend towards strong associational models in the suburban Church of England churches, where the grouping factor may be church tradition or style of worship and which, although attractive to their gathered congregations, isolate those who do not feel they belong there, *even though* the parochial system locates them at those churches.

1.81 In the inner city, the Church may have of necessity to use a much more open model. A Church Centre, for example, may have a multiplicity of functions including health care and social services, building up a variety of 'belongings' which may or may not be religious. In some Urban Priority Areas the concept of church *qua* church may simply be too much of a luxury. In other cases, we may look at the example of the St Marylebone Healing and Counselling Centre in London, which offers an NHS practice and up-to-date medical technology as well as alternative therapies, healing and spiritual direction and which is located in a functioning church with the Director as part of the clergy staff. The Centre also has a restaurant. This leads us to ask what bridges there are for people to cross from participation in social and health care over to what is offered by the Church in its worship, fellowship, spiritual direction and teaching. Surely, then, hospitality is an important aspect of mission.

The Body of Christ

1.82 While sociological and anthropological views of believing and belonging may give important insights into religious behaviour, it is also necessary to look at theological perspectives of belonging. In one important sense, the Church is the community of all baptised Christians and all who are baptised are invested with a belonging which is inescapably part of their identity and which may bring them to church at major intersections in their lives. The Church is also the community of dedicated people who belong, of identified Christians who have made public profession of their belief, and of those who regularly attend church or who are on membership rolls.

1.83   Theologically, the Body of Christ (see 1 Corinthians 12; Romans 12) is one image of the Christian Church and as such it is assumed to be whole, an inclusive society, even though visibly fragmented denominationally and by the fracture between the communal and associational membership of those who participate and those who do not. This brings us back to Susan Hope's point, in the story about Terry the out-of-work boxer, whether there is a difference between being 'in Christ' and 'in the Body of Christ' which can be expressed as a continuum of strength of commitment.

1.84   This leaves us with the implications for belonging brought about by movements for Christian unity such as Churches Together bodies and other ecumenical projects and by the acceptance of the principle of unity in diversity and Christian diversity within plurality. With the general fragmentation of traditional core groupings in modern society it is clear that the strengthening of belief systems cannot be sustained by the notion of belonging. Consequently, working out what it means to be the Body of Christ in a whole series of fragmentations is a complex theological task. It may be that the Church is required to redefine what it means by *koinonia*, by fellowship, perhaps in terms of 'moral communities'. The problem with the latter is that there will also be diversity in how a church or congregation can form and express itself as a moral community.[46] The Church may need to address how far it desires Christians to stand over against society and in judgement of it. Agreed understandings of this may form part of belief–belonging interaction in a congregation, but this will vary.

1.85   *Koinonia*, fellowship, may be seen to operate under a double function. Love, tolerance, self-giving may be particular qualities which bind religious groups together as a community, and increase the sense of belonging through believing that this is the way to behave under God. Further, these aspects of a 'moral community' may also be what marks out a religious fellowship from other groups and networks, and should be particularly evident in Christian congregations, whatever their diversity. This is surely important for mission.

1.86 Again, the missionary possibilities of congregations which are seen as moral communities may depend on the permeability of boundaries. In some cases, might not the strength of belonging to the community mean exclusion for those who would call themselves Christian but fall short of the group's interpretation of the biblical ideal? Recent examples which highlight this question include the refusal of a homosexual person as a godparent in one church and the isolation of adulterous church members in another. Other, 'softer' groups might seek to include those whom they would perceive to fall short, at the risk of appearing themselves undiscriminating or hypocritical.

1.87 In each of the two cases, different mission strategies would be implied by the type of *koinonia* the group wished to sustain. The first might insist on an outreach programme which saw conversion and repentance taking place outside the group as a result of witness by example. The second might take a 'judge not that you be not judged' attitude, expecting those admitted to the fellowship to be affected positively by becoming part of the group. Each type of moral community would also be placed to receive a certain type of person. The first would attract those desiring to make a complete transformation, leaving the old life behind; the second would attract those wishing to bring their lives and consciousness of brokenness into the fellowship itself. In each case, the group's perception of itself as fellowship, its self-description as a moral community and the way it communicates this to others have important implications for the way it can act in mission effectively.

1.88 When we say that the Church exists as a set of moral communities, this, together with other faith communities, gives religious institutions a corporate voice and power to stand over against the moral pluralism or 'anything goes' mentality of modern society. For Christians, the Body of Christ preserves the vision of ideals which make it possible for God's kingdom to exist. In order for God's future to come about, the Church has to preserve an image of a various community life lived according to God's intention. In doing so, it is able publicly to exercise judgement and to wait for society's tendency to fragment to return towards a search for coherence. As Archbishop Aram Keshishian has said:

> Mission is not merely a function of *Koinonia* – it is her very *raison d'être*. The church has no mission. She participates in the *missio Dei*. God's will revealed in Jesus Christ calls the churches to common witness and service for the renewal of the world from its brokenness .... The church is called to break down barriers and reconcile a broken humanity. Thus the church as reconciled and reconciling *Koinonia* should express in her own life and mission God's purpose for humanity and creation.[47]

1.89 This emphasis on the reconciling power of *koinonia* points us to a way through the problems of living in a diverse Church in a morally pluralistic world. Christians draw on their experience of fellowship within a local context of believing and belonging to forge strong bonds with others within and outside the Church. *Koinonia* is strengthened as reconciling work is done. In this way, each person in the fellowship contributes to the witness of the Church.

Conclusion

1.90 This brings us back to the basic common denominator: the person, known, chosen and loved by God before birth, cherished by God in relationship with God. We need to find out how we can recover the notion of belonging to God in ways which map on to the way life is lived in modern society. For example, if as is sometimes suggested, the 'post-modern' condition is characterised by fragmentation, then perhaps God can be found, fragmented and scattered, each fragment to be reconstituted whole for those searching for faith, wherever it is found. This notion of the *Logos Spermatikos*, the Scattered Word, which goes back to Justin Martyr, may be helpful in defining a mission strategy for the whole Church. The bread broken for us in the eucharist is gathered up into one in the solidarity of the eucharistic community: 'Though we are many, we are one Body, for we all partake of the one bread.' Further, this move towards solidarity is also a mission act, since it strengthens the Church in the recognition of its oneness under God. It is up to the Church, then, to find new methods of incorporating people into ways of belonging which do not conflict with their modes of belonging to other things. There have to be new openings which allow people to experience this community of the faithful in ways which are meaningful to them.

1.91 In creating these new openings, we must activate *koinonia* in ways which serve and complement the needs of particular kinds of people. We must also find new ways of being sacramental and of enabling the disenfranchised individual to belong. It is a human instinct to search for satisfying methods of belonging and a mirror of the totally interpersonal belonging that is characteristic of the Trinity. None the less, belonging cannot be imposed. Belonging can carry with it a fierce rightness and zeal, while its converse, not-belonging, can be alienating and painful. Consequently, we might usefully consider first not how people believe, but how they belong. In this way we can look again at how we act in mission and share our faith.

Summary

KEY WORDS

- believing
- belonging
- faith
- baptism
- individualisation
- post-materialism
- networks
- covenant
- fellowship

Religious belief in Britain remains relatively high, while belonging to the Church has declined. Believing and belonging are interrelated concepts and while sociologists differ as to how these are linked, there is now an emphasis on commitment as an index for believing and belonging in society.

Baptism remains the normative criterion for belonging in the Christian Church, but there are growing numbers of unbaptised. Even where people are not baptised as infants, the average time it takes for a person to come to a public profession of faith is four years. What kinds of belonging are available to people whose search for faith does not come by these routes? Scripture shows that Christian belief may be about belonging, as much as about believing. Covenant and fellowship are key concepts.

We have to take account of the process of individualisation and a strong pre-eminent sense of identity, over against ideas of relationism. This goes along with post-materialism, the emphasis on choice and on quality of life. A person may have dispersed geographical landmarks which are important and which relate to a set of dispersed networks. There are also various notions of belonging to a family in modern society. There are also changes in the way people participate or exercise membership, with a shift to nonactive, or non-committed belonging, resulting in people's experiences becoming distant and isolating. Some religious groupings become closed, separating out belonging to the group and belonging to the world. This is also true of some businesses and work environments.

It is necessary to distinguish the kinds of belonging available in the mainstream denominations and what bridges there are to those who do not belong to a church or fellowship. This means working out what it means to be the Body of Christ and what modes of belonging are available to people experiencing modern life and the trends of modern society. The mission question is how the Church can make it possible for such people to feel they can belong.

Further reading

Barton, Stephen C. (ed.), *The Family in Theological Perspective*, T. & T. Clark, 1996.

Bruce, Steve, *Religion in Modern Britain*, OUP, 1995.

Davie, Grace, *Religion in Britain Since 1945: Believing without Belonging*, in the *Making Contemporary Britain* series, Blackwell, 1994.

Finney, John, *Finding Faith Today: How Does it Happen?* British and Foreign Bible Society, 1992.

Gill, Robin, *The Myth of the Empty Church*, SPCK, 1993.

Something to Celebrate: Valuing Families in Church and Society, CHP, 1995.

Things to do

- **AIM:** to help you think about how people belong
  - in your local area
  - to your church or group
- **PURPOSE:** to see the points of contact between your church or group and the local community.

The Search for Faith

BIBLE VERSE

> Let us therefore no longer pass judgement on one another, but resolve instead never to put a stumbling block or hindrance in the way of another. (Romans 14.13)

Things to do include:

a. A story to read, think about and discuss
b. A plan for drawing your own map of where you go and belong
c. Some discussion starters.

1. A STORY

Take me to your leader

Imagine a friendly alien has been observing our planet from his capsule. The capsule is characterised by a highly individualised lifestyle and has everything technology can provide to make the inhabitant comfortable: computer systems, TV, Internet, videos, CDs, microwave, washing machine (with multiple functions), a gym. The alien is alone but never lonely for he can chat to his friends using satellite communications. He knows via a multiplicity of channels what is happening on the earth. He supports a particular football team and belongs to a number of societies by using his electronic communications. He feels he is reasonably fulfilled and would be called 'post-materialist' for he has a high quality of life – *but does he belong to this planet?*

When the alien stops to consider such things, he thinks that all in all he does believe in God. Indeed, he is not above talking to God when things go wrong, or when the shadow side of his comfortable life intervenes.

One day the alien does something rather unusual. He leaves the capsule and goes to an unfamiliar place where human beings are gathered together. He goes in and is overwhelmed by the numbers of people sitting in rows. He ventures to sit down, but Mrs Brown always sits there and, sorry, Mandy's friend will be along in a minute. He finds an empty space uncomfortably near the front and works out that he should have equipped himself at the door with a red book, a green book and a sheet.

Something is happening and everyone but him knows what to do, when to stand, sit, sing. He can just about follow the book, but bits keep getting missed out and other bits mysteriously put in, so he spends his time catching up – a stranger who stands out. How is he ever going to learn what to do? He is left standing when the others are sitting down and feels embarrassed. Suddenly there is hand-shaking – thirty seconds of intense attention. What was that for?

Now he is asked for money, but he doesn't have any and his credit card won't do. Now everyone's getting up and going to the front. Why? He sits still and people stare. He feels envious of the people who know the drill, but how much effort is it going to take to achieve that level of familiarity? Where is there a book that will help him make sense of it all?

On the way out most people are friendly but still manage to pretend he doesn't exist. There is coffee in the hall but he can't bear the agony of standing out as an alien. Is the urge that brought him here enough to bring him back again, or to try somewhere else?

He goes back to his capsule and turns on the TV. *Neighbours* is on. Thank God.

Questions

- What is happening in this story?
- How do we treat non-church members – like people from another planet?

Could you retell this story as if the church were an alien spaceship and the incomer had been captured by aliens? Think back to a time when you entered an unfamiliar place. What were your feelings? What helped you to feel that you belonged? Have you been back since?

The Search for Faith

Figure 3 Networks

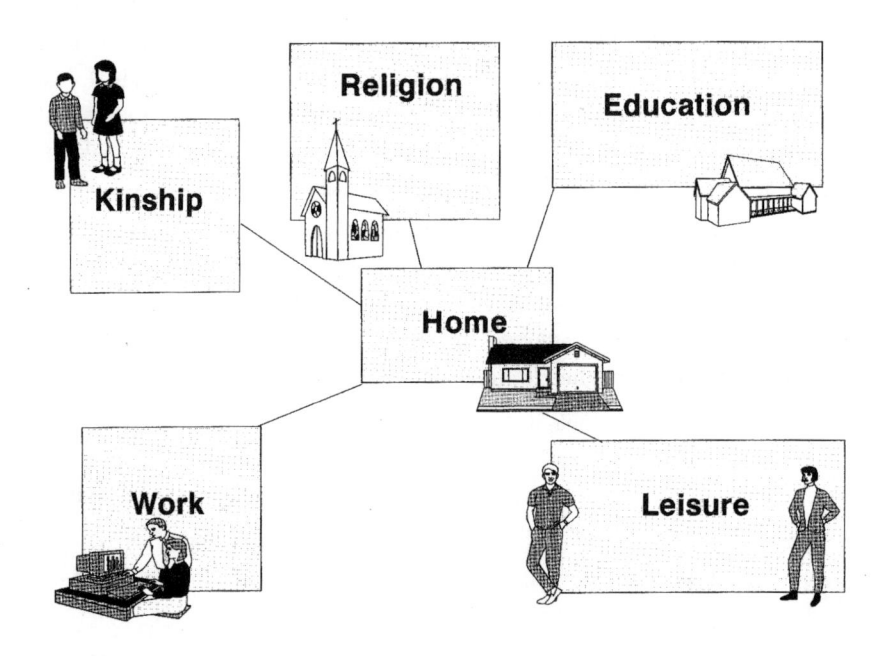

[Diagram showing networks: Kinship, Religion, Education, Home, Work, Leisure]

2. LANDMARKS

Divide into groups, preferably of those who live near one another. Use the landmarks sheet to draw a map of where you go every day. Compare this with other people's maps. Where are your opportunities for meeting people? How many of them are outside the church?

3. SOME DISCUSSION QUESTIONS

Choose a question from the list of discussion questions below that is relevant to your situation. This can be done in pairs. Ask each pair to discuss the question generally and then contribute two ideas at the end of the discussion period. Write these up on a flipchart. Use these ideas with the whole group to get a picture of what you can learn or do in response to the question.

Figure 4 Geographical landmarks

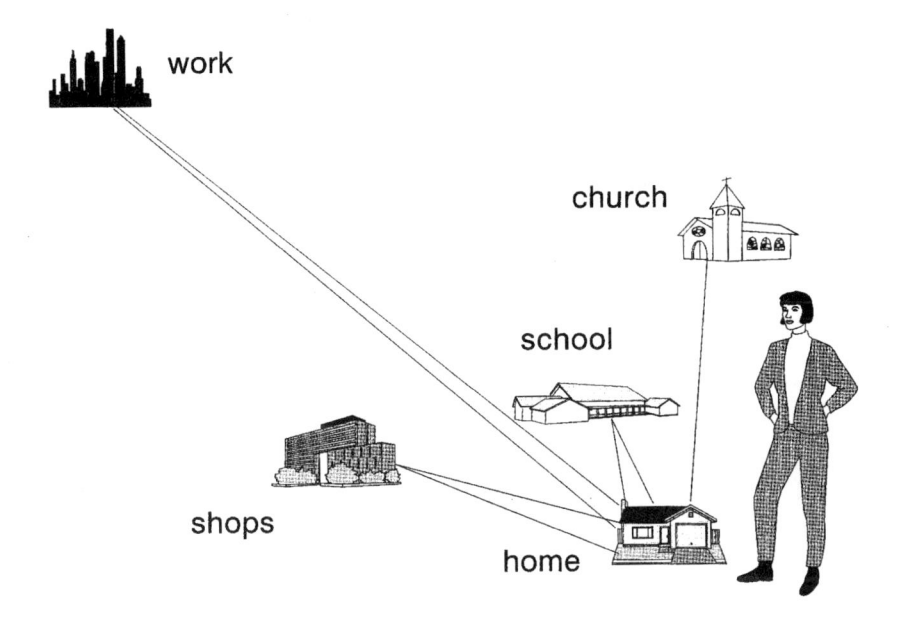

- work
- church
- school
- shops
- home

a. In your opinion, do churches care more about those who pay for the church to be maintained, or about those searching for faith outside?

b. Do you think baptism is about believing, belonging, or both? Do you have a baptism policy which reflects this? Are there ever grounds for refusal? If so, why?

c. What can we learn from people who decide *not* to join the Church? Are there people *we* don't want to join the Church? Why?

d. What role does 'doubting Thomas' have to play in the Church? What does Peter's denial and faith tell us about those searching for God and about ourselves?

e. Is it important if the church turns out *not* to be the centre of our personal map?

f. Where do you think your church is on the diagram of believing and belonging? Where do you think your mission opportunities are?

g. Are networks more important than neighbourhoods in your area? How can your church make use of relevant networks?

Notes

1. Grace Davie, paper for the Doctrine Commission of the General Synod of the Church of England.
2. See Grace Davie, *Religion in Britain Since 1945: Believing without Belonging*, in the *Making Contemporary Britain* series, Blackwell, 1994, p.78. Results from Robert Towler's research 'Conventional religion and common religion in Leeds' and published in H. Krarup, *Conventional Religion and Common Religion in Leeds: Interview Schedule*, University of Leeds, 1983, include: 72 per cent of those surveyed said they believed in God (p.46); 71 per cent prayed (p.64); 76 per cent claimed to have a religion but only 30 per cent attended a place of worship.
3. Davie, op. cit., p.79. The diversity of religious experience is well attested by the various research documents from the Alister Hardy Research Centre in Oxford, some of which will be examined in other chapters of this report.
4. Davie, op. cit., p.2.
5. See Robin Gill, *The Myth of the Empty Church*, SPCK, 1993. Gill outlines what he sees as a consensus of opinion among sociologists concerning reasons for church-going decline and lists these on pp.2–3. His counter-propositions are given on pp.9–12. In chapter 8, he also examines diachronic data concerning decline in the twentieth century, on the premise that if the 'empty church' is inherited from structural problems in the nineteenth century, decline would appear to be inevitable: 'At many levels the empty church feeds the empty church' (p.190).
6. Paul Handley, 'Faith and Reason', *Independent*, 28 October 1995, p.14.
7. Margaret Drabble, *The Millstone*, Penguin edition, 1968, pp.126–7.
8. Quoted by Clifford Longley in 'A Message from the Voters', *Spotlight* section, *The Tablet*, 2 December 1995.
9. *Christian Initiation and Church Membership*, BCC, 1988, p.25.
10. See *Good News in our Times: The Gospel and Contemporary Cultures*, CHP, 1991, chapter 10.
11. *Baptism, Eucharist and Ministry*, Faith and Order paper no. 111, WCC, 1982, p.3.
12. *Christian Initiation and Church Membership*, op. cit., p. 25.
13. *The Alternative Service Book*, OUP, 1980, p.243.
14. Ibid.
15. Also see *On the Way: Towards an Integrated Approach to Christian Initiation*, CHP, 1995.
16. *Initiation Services*, a report by the Liturgical Commission of the General Synod of the Church of England, GS 1152, p.47.

17. 'Me and My God', Kathleen Hale talks to Frances Welch, *Sunday Telegraph Review*, 26 February 1995. Despite her son's perception, see note 20 below.
18. David Winter, 'Diary' in the *Church Times*, 9 June 1995.
19. See *Anglican Marriage in England and Wales: A Guide to the Law for Clergy*, from the Faculty Office of the Archbishop of Canterbury, 6:6.1–6.2, pp.15–16, viz.: 'In England every resident of a parish is entitled to marry in his/her parish church.' The exceptions to this do not include the unbaptised: 'the fact that a party (or both parties) are unbaptised does not deprive them of the right to marry after banns'.
20. David Winter, 'Diary' in the *Church Times*, 11 August 1995.
21. *Finding Faith Today*, op. cit.
22. Ibid., p.25.
23. Susan Hope, 'Sanctuary', in *God in the City*, Mowbray, 1995, p.195.
24. The Archbishop of Canterbury in Mary Loudon, *Revelations: The Clergy Questioned*, Penguin edition, 1995, pp.262–3.
25. And see ARCIC, *The Final Report*, Windsor, September 1981, SPCK/CTS, 1982, p.83.
26. Oliver Sacks, *The Man who Mistook his Wife for a Hat*, Picador edition, 1986, p.36.
27. Martin Buber, *I and Thou*, (1923) English edition, R. R. Clark, 1937.
28. Professor Ruud de Moor in *The European Value Systems Study 1981–1990*, summary report, European Values Group, Gordon Clarke Foundation, 1992, pp.6, 10.
29. For an exploration of Spencer's ideas, see Kenneth Pople, *Stanley Spencer*, Collins, 1991.
30. Brian Keenan, *An Evil Cradling*, Vintage edition, 1993, p.76.
31. *The Mystery of Salvation: The Story of God's Gift*, a report by the Doctrine Commission of the General Synod of the Church of England, CHP, 1995, p.142.
32. Alistair McFadyen, *The Call to Personhood*, CUP, 1990. Also compare the work of J. Zizioulas in *Being as Communion*, Darton, Longman and Todd, 1985.
33. 'Autism as a subject touches on the deepest questions of ontology, for it involves a radical deviation in the development of brain and mind' (Oliver Sacks, *An Anthropologist on Mars*, Picador edition, 1995, p.235).
34. Ibid., p.248.
35. See Bishop Michael Nazir-Ali, *Mission and Dialogue: Proclaiming the Gospel Afresh in Every Age*, SPCK, 1995, pp.6–7.
36. This phrase is sometimes used to describe the 'shop-around' ideas of post-modern culture. See, for example, Graham Cray, *From Here to Where: The Culture of the Nineties*, Board of Mission Occasional Paper, Number 3, 1992.
37. See Finney, op. cit., chapter 4.
38. Martin Robinson, *The Faith of the Unbeliever*, Monarch, 1994, p.87.
39. For an examination of this see *Something to Celebrate: Valuing Families in Church and Society*, CHP, 1995.
40. Although the European Value Systems Study group detected a slight swing towards the 'traditional' pattern of family in its study, there are currently in Britain a number of

The Search for Faith

challenges to the supremacy of the nuclear family: 'the nuclear family is seen by too many as too stifling, secretive and imprisoning .... The family may be important in the world, but Jesus ... is surely a corrective to any tendency to give it inflated importance.' Christine McMullen, writing in *Home and Family*, the magazine of the Mothers' Union.

41. An example might be the practice in some churches of giving flowers to mothers on Mothering Sunday and thereby ignoring the role of single fathers, devoted aunts and other carers in the nurture and care of children within the family.
42. *Breaking New Ground: Church Planting in the Church of England*, CHP, 1994, p.3.
43. For a discussion of this, see Greg Smith, 'You and Who Else' (the 'C' Word) in *Third Way*, February 1995, pp.21–4.
44. Catherine Shelley, 'A welcome kind of crisis', *Face to faith* section, the *Guardian*, 22 June 1996.
45. Lavinia Byrne in Mary Loudon, *Unveiled: Nuns Talking*, Chatto and Windus, 1992, p.149.
46. See Robin Gill, *Moral Communities*, Exeter University Press, 1992.
47. Archbishop Aram Keshishian, *Growing Together Towards a Full Koinonia*, in the Moderator's report to the WCC Central Committee, August 1992.

2

Pearls are for tears . . .

My name's Jenny. When I get up in the morning, I say a little prayer to the good spirits, just to make it a good day. It's not that serious. I know that there's something important at the bottom of it all, but it's deep down. It only comes out when something happens to shock you out of the ordinary way of seeing things, like those little children in Dunblane.

I do go up to the church sometimes because my nan's buried there. I go and tell her what I'm worried about and maybe tidy up the grave a bit. It gives me a sense of peace doing that. I'm sure the dead are watching out for us and keeping us away from the bad things. Sometimes I think I can hear her saying comforting things to me and that makes me feel good.

I never actually go in the church though. It's not really necessary, is it? As like as you keep to the side of the good, like taking your baby to be done, that's all you need, isn't it ...

Introduction

Implicit religion can include both 'folk' or 'popular' religion as well as 'civic' religion. It can be characterised by religious ideas and concepts which are embedded in history and culture and expressed by the deeply felt need in people to enact rituals and have 'sacred occasions'. How does the Church meet these needs and respond to them?

Superstitious beliefs and behaviour based on superstitious feelings about the world demonstrate how people feel the need to stay on the side of the good and ward off the bad. The Church is challenged to provide an understanding of Christian faith which releases people from superstitious anxiety and offers peace and reconciliation.

The Search for Faith

The occasional offices of the Church, especially baptism, marriage and funerals, often provide occasions where the implicit religious awareness of people comes to the surface and is strongly expressed. How can the Church react sensitively to people's implicit religion on these occasions while still maintaining its duty to make sure the sacraments are not abused?

Occasions of civic religion, especially at times of national mourning, such as attended the Hillsborough tragedy or the murders in Dunblane, can expose powerful religious needs to which the Church is required to respond. Other kinds of civic occasion also provide opportunities for the Church to help bring out people's implicit belief, and may represent issues important not only to Christians, but also to other world faiths.

Challenges from implicit religion

2.1 In Chapter 1, we discussed the important interaction between believing and belonging, which finds many of those who are searching for faith left outside the Church when it cannot offer them a mode of belonging that makes sense to them. In this chapter and in Chapter 3, we look at two sorts of believing which go on inside and outside the structures and institutions of formal religion. In this chapter, we look at the deep down elements, often buried inside a person's search for faith. In Chapter 3, we look more closely at overt and systematised expressions of people's spiritual lives, for both implicit religion and contemporary spirituality challenge the Church about what it offers those searching for faith. Some of the stories and material contained in the previous chapter have a particular relevance in this and in the next, and to this extent, Chapters 1–3 may be said to fit together and form a cluster around similar issues.

2.2 When the Church of England Doctrine Commission published its report *The Mystery of Salvation* in January 1996, public interest in its pronouncements about the nature of hell was quite remarkable. Even though less than 14 per cent of the population regularly attend church,[1] many national newspapers commented upon the report's findings about hell and *The Times*, *Telegraph* and *Independent* regarded the subject of sufficient significance to write about it in their editorial columns. As we saw in the previous chapter, this reaction indicates a greater interest in some areas of faith and belief than church attendance figures would suggest. Indeed, it is a consistent finding in surveys about belief in Britain that there is a widespread belief in God, though the nature of that belief varies greatly. In the 1991 British Social Attitudes Survey, only 10 per cent of the population claimed to be atheists and 13 per cent took an agnostic position and the rest (over 75 per cent) acknowledged some kind of belief in some kind of God.[2]

2.3   In the last chapter, we considered the existence of this 'drifting belief' in terms of its relation to belonging, but we also have to consider it in terms of 'postponed decision'. The search for faith may be crowded out by the practicalities of modern living, but elements of a belief system are strongly embedded as religious feelings and ideas both in language and culture: the former can be seen in such throw-away phrases as 'Thank God for small mercies' and 'Heaven help me'; the latter is exemplified in the relationship between Church and State, which has ramifications at every level of society. Furthermore, the close association between belief and culture is underlined when one remembers that the word 'culture' is derived from the Latin *colere* which means to worship. This implies that the worship of *something* binds together the people who make up a culture.

2.4   The depth and extent of religious feeling are seen in the way that it can bubble up spontaneously, even among people with so-called secular lifestyles, at times of thanksgiving and disaster (both local and national), and at times of personal milestones such as birth, marriage and death. The Alister Hardy Research Centre has discovered from surveys it has conducted that around one third of the adult population of Britain are prepared to admit that they have been aware of some presence or power, usually interpreted religiously, which has at some time entered into their lives.[3] We shall further explore some of the Centre's findings in the following chapter. This religious consciousness, which is frequently unarticulated and is a phenomenon shared by all who believe, both inside and outside formal religious structures, is commonly called implicit or folk religion. It is the purpose of this chapter to explore what is understood by implicit religion, to reflect upon the dynamics of the relationship between it and formal Christianity and then to suggest a response from the point of view of mission.

The Search for Faith

Exploring implicit religion

2.5 We will use the term implicit religion in this chapter to refer to the religious consciousness described in the foregoing paragraph. However, this religious consciousness reveals itself in a number of different ways and so under the category of implicit religion there is 'popular' or 'folk' religion (we shall be using the word 'folk') and there is 'civic' religion.

2.6 Although this chapter will be concentrating on the relationship of folk or implicit religion to formal Christianity, it is important to be aware that a similar dynamic exists with other world religions. Hinduism, Buddhism and Islam have 'folk' elements too.

2.7 Folk religion is an *ad hoc* mixture of formal religion and local beliefs. It is a set of loosely related practices, often mutually contradictory, used not to present a coherent view of reality, but to produce immediate results and to offer strategies for living. It provides, for example, various courses of action for those facing immediate problems such as illness, bad fortune and sudden deaths; for those seeking success in love, in winning chance games such as the National Lottery and in passing exams; and for those wanting guidance in making important decisions.[4] It suggests ways in which one can ward off the bad and align oneself to the good.

2.8 Anthropologist Clifford Geertz compares folk religion to the inner parts of an old city with its narrow winding streets, dark corners and many little shops where there is often little apparent order, yet much is going on.[5] People of many kinds crowd the lanes and fill the cafés with laughter and animated gossip. Formal religion, on the other hand, is like the suburbs surrounding the inner city with their neatly laid-out streets and spacious houses arranged in precise order. Here life is more sedate and peaceful; and sometimes those living here venture into the inner city for its excitement and colour. Folk religion seeks immediate answers to particular situations, whereas formal religion deals with cosmic questions facing humanity regarding the meaning and end of this world and the ultimate meaning of life. If people feel that their needs and questions are not being taken seriously or cannot be met by formal religion, then they may turn to alternative religions or practices such as astrology, the reading of tarot cards and fortune-telling.

2.9 One of the ways implicit religion can manifest itself is through rituals. In general, human beings need ritual to help them encounter the mysterious and the incomprehensible and to enable them to move on from such an encounter. Ritual makes connections between meaning and making. Hans-Gunther Heimbrock, drawing on the work of the social anthropologist Mary Douglas, alludes to her definitions of rituals as 'restricted code' in which there is 'a more rigid ordering of linguistic patterns, a higher degree of particularity, contextuality, and a higher count of non-verbal elements'. Douglas, however, sees social preference being given to 'elaborate code' in which 'the rational, explicitly verbal and personal relation to God is more highly developed'. Suppression of rituals in favour of rational and articulate religiosity contains 'seeds of alienation'. Heimbrock concludes:

> Coupled with the loss of the ritual dimension is the loss of that dimension of religious communication which satisfies the life-long need of persons to grasp things in non-verbal fashion as well as their recurring and by no means infantile yearning for an overcoming of the deeply ingrained boundaries between 'interior' and 'exterior' which they perceive in their everyday experiences.[6]

2.10 So Madeleine Bunting comments:

> The role of ritual was to inspire and then formulate our response to the sacred. With so little appreciation for the latter, it's not surprising that we have largely junked the regular practice of rituals which have been a feature of human society for thousands of years. We seem to manage very well without them, you might say. But where it all collapses is in those great life events, when even the most hardened sceptics find themselves floundering to find a ritual which will express the profundity of the experience, and this is the important point, expresses the event's life-changing significance – which places it on a different level from our daily mundane preoccupations.[7]

2.11 Some significant rituals, which previously were imbued with powerful symbolic value, still survive in various forms today, such as dancing round the Maypole and the crowning of the May Queen. J. G. Frazer's famous study quotes W. Mannhardt, an authority on vegetation rituals:

We may conclude that these begging processions with May-trees or May boughs from door to door ('bringing the May or the summer') had everywhere originally a serious and, so to speak, sacramental significance; people really believed that the god of growth was present unseen in the bough; by the procession he was brought to each house to bestow his blessing. The names Father May, May Lady, Queen of the May, by which the anthropomorphic spirit of vegetation is often denoted, show that the idea of the spirit of vegetation is blent with a personification of the season at which his powers are most strikingly manifested.[8]

2.12 Rituals become particularly necessary at milestones in people's lives, as Bunting points out. The May rituals were associated with sexuality, fertility and fruitfulness. So in some European rural societies even today, a boy at puberty may be taken to the woods and passed through the two halves of a split sapling while prayers are said. The sapling is then bound up again and, as it continues to grow and flourish, so does the boy-become-a-man.[9] Such rites of passage can have a tremendous hold and significance on those whose faith is not located in a particular religious context, and it is here that the rites and sacraments of the Church may have much to offer.

2.13 For example, the rite of baptism enables an encounter with the mystery of creation and marks a new beginning. We noted in the previous chapter that the birth of a baby may encourage a flood of religious feelings expressed as gratitude and wonder. Such feelings may well prompt the request for baptism and find a home in its ceremonial. A new-born baby will bring parents asking for baptism even though they find it difficult to articulate precisely why they want their baby baptised. Such comments as 'I want her to be baptised so that she will go to heaven if she dies' and 'My mother thought he should be done' are frequently expressions of a deeply held unarticulated belief and need to belong, with which many practising Christians would identify. The Church would want to speak of baptism as incorporation into the death and resurrection of Jesus Christ and membership of the Christian community: the challenge to formal religion is how far it can interact with the local needs in the way suggested in the previous paragraph so that both are renewed and challenged by the encounter with Christ. Mircea Eliade, who has done much study and research in this area, writes in his book *Images and Symbols*:

By its renewal of the great figures and symbolizations of natural religion, Christianity has also renewed their vitality and their power in the depths of the psyche .... The adoption by Christ and the church of the great images of the sun, the moon, of wood, water, the sea and so forth amounts to an evangelization of the effective powers that they denote. The Incarnation must not be reduced to the taking of flesh alone. God has intervened even in the collective unconscious, that it may be saved and fulfilled.[10]

2.14 The Roman Catholic writer and artist David Jones makes the point in his writings that elements of the natural world such as water, wood and stone, become conveyors of the holy and structures in God's plan of salvation: baptism, cross, altar.[11] So the recognition of what is numinous in nature at the folk religion level is raised through increasing consciousness of God's activity to find its ultimate expression in Jesus's life and death and in the sacraments of the Church. The challenge to the Church is to help people understand the transition from the basic elements to the sacramental reality. We should not assume that this is either easy or automatic for people whose relevant signs and symbols may be quite other than the traditional ones.

2.15 Marriage represents another place where implicit religion bubbles to the surface. When so much attention is paid to the bride's make-up preparation, white dress and veil, attendants, flowers, rings, confetti, and cake, this may pass to attention to the liturgical parts of the whole ritual: the music, vows and prayers. Because so much attention and energy is typically focused on a wedding day, this represents a particular opportunity for the Church to leave a deep impression of joy and completeness. Marriage will bring couples seeking the Church's blessing and affirmation on their union. The location and beauty of a building may be a factor that encourages them to decide in favour of the Church rather than the Registry Office; they may feel that their marriage stands a better chance of working if it is blessed by God; but the religious potential within such a situation should not be underestimated. Moreover, in view of a recent debate in the media about whether it is proper to hold 'divorce' rituals in church, we have to spend time trying to understand what kind of faith (implicit or otherwise) drives people back to the Church at crisis points in their lives and what we offer them when they do.

2.16 The laying of hands on sick people is a sign of the mutual recognition of illness which may open up a way forward in which the progression of the illness is accepted or resisted. People who feel their peace of mind disturbed in some way may find laying on of hands or anointing within a liturgical setting successfully allows their spiritual feeling to be addressed.

2.17 Death too is the occasion for an encounter with formal religion. When the bereaved are surrounded by fear and uncertainty, the Church provides a link with the inexpressible, unfathomable and mysterious and offers hope and the possibility that there is meaning to life and death. In many villages one often finds more people attending the graves of their loved ones in the churchyard on a Saturday than attending services in church on Sunday. It is often easier to collect money for the upkeep of the village churchyard than for the upkeep of the Church.

2.18 The following illustration explores the interest in churchyards:

> As a minister, I would feel slightly less than charitable to those who were coming to the churchyard to tend family graves while I was leaving the church after worship. Now I have come to a new understanding of the faithfulness of those who bring fresh flowers on special occasions, even all year round. It may be that more people use the churchyard round the year than come to the church building .... I also became interested in what people were doing (internally, as well as externally), when they 'did' the graves. At its simplest, they 'put things straight', and then placed their flowers there. But I could also see they checked their arrangement, and its positioning, to make sure they were 'just right' and then paused.
>
> People said they had 'a little think' or even 'a little talk' with the one for whom they still cared .... Then the parallel dawned. The tending of the grave may be compared to the reading and exposition of scripture; the offering of the flowers which are both gift and sacrifice provides the way to a moment of communion with the recipient. So the churchyard is a gathering point like the wayside shrines found in so many countries. The grave becomes an altar, set aside for a ritual sacrifice which is the place for a spiritual communion.[12]

2.19 Here, Edward Bailey discovers a contingent belonging in which people enact rituals in the environs of the church but not actually within it. Relationship, here, is all important and provides the gateway for religious expression in ways in which the participants feel comfortable. It is interesting to note that in the BBC soap opera *EastEnders*, Michelle, troubled about having to make a decision whether or not to go to America, went to have 'a little talk' with her grandmother at her grave. Her grandmother's friend Ethel, also come to the graveyard to be close to her friend, offers to help Michelle by reading her tea leaves. The tea leaves offer her conventional domesticity. Michelle, rejecting projected hopes and superstitious practice, draws on her relationship with her grandmother and, seeing more clearly, leaves for America.[13] Edward Bailey's gravetenders and Michelle require, like the poet Philip Larkin, a sacrament of the personalised ritual. In 'Church Going', Philip Larkin writes that he is drawn to churches but will enter only when 'there's nothing going on' and is moved to meditation, if not by what the Church teaches then by the fact that 'so many dead lie round'.

2.20 Yet even Philip Larkin, who spent much time meditating on 'The sure extinction that we travel to/And shall be lost in always' ('Aubade'), strikes a different note when contemplating the effigies on a tomb. What for him proves 'Our almost-instinct almost true' is the idea that 'what will survive of us is love' ('An Arundel Tomb').[14] The placing of coins in the hand or mouth of a dead person enables the bereaved to feel that they have provided payment for the 'journey' of the deceased and they can now allow them to go. The sense that the bereaved have to be reassured that the dead have got safely through to the afterlife is particularly powerful and can override both the intellectual acceptance of dissolution in Buddhism, as well as trenchant atheism.

2.21 This highlights the importance of memory and continuity in people's lives. Believing may become important precisely because this continuity of belonging means something to people. We can see this where some cultures have annexed Christian worship to their traditional ancestor worship.

> Recourse to them [the ancestors] is made not only to ask some favour, such as a cure or the satisfaction of some need, but also, simply in order to remember them – as a memorial, to perpetuate a memory, a history of deeds and words, an experience of the victory of life over death. Recourse to the Ancestors, whatever its nature or occasion, is always a source of blessing.[15]

The Search for Faith

2.22   Japanese Christians may have the names of their ancestors pinned to the vestry wall, and hold memorial services for these ancestors. In Ghana, the local religious practice of pouring beer over the graves of the dead has been changed through the encounter with Christianity into a eucharistic celebration. Similarly, in the west, occasions like All Souls Day and Remembrance Sunday provide particular opportunities for the Church to open windows onto this aspect of people's need. Similarly, *In Memoriam* notices posted in local papers testify to a need to retain the sense of belonging to the dead person and the hope to be reunited with them in restored relationship. In some hospitals, there may be a service for all who have died there in the past year.

2.23   We may see here, and will discuss below, the importance of acknowledging the love relationship which is occasioned by birth, marriage and death. People's consciousness of love in their relationships may be precisely what opens them to be receptive to God's love and allows them to conceive of relationship with God (cf. John 13.34; 15.12; 1 John 4.7). Understanding how love makes people receptive to the gospel is of particular importance to the Church's response to those who have not made a religious commitment.

2.24   One way in which the Church might address people's needs for rituals in daily life is to use versions of home liturgy. This is common in parts of the Anglican Communion, but celebration of events such as the coming home of a new baby, New Year's day, birthdays, anniversaries, death-days, have tended to become secular occasions in the west. The provision of a short ritual to bring secular celebrations into religious settings and thereby to familiarise people with praying together and offering thanks to God can be a powerful way of bringing the sacred into a special occasion.[16]

2.25   Ritual can also provide protection from evil. Thus, for some people it is important that their child is baptised as soon as possible because they believe that if the child were to die unbaptised he or she would not go to heaven. One of the functions of religion, both formal and folk, is to provide both the ritual and its meaning. We have noted that people often post *In Memoriam* notices in the local paper, and these often invoke safety for the dead loved one through the continued love and memory of the relatives. The Church can provide its own place of safety for these memories and should perhaps help people find the words to express their sentiments, rather than the local paper.

2.26 We can see, then, that there are occasions when the needs of folk religion can be met by the Church. Non-attenders do frequently approach their local church for its support and blessing in the rites of passage of birth, marriage and death. It may be argued that people are seeking public recognition and affirmation of the important threshold that they have reached: in other words, they seek, through baptism, communal recognition of the new birth; through marriage, communal recognition of a new relationship; and through a funeral, communal recognition of having to face a new future without the deceased. Indeed, Christianity takes root more deeply in a culture when Christians listen seriously to local beliefs and myths, struggle to discover where God is already at work in that culture and then, in humility, enable the loving and judging light of Christ to love and judge that culture and themselves.[17]

2.27 Civic religion is another manifestation of implicit religion. In civic religion Church and State share a common religious expression, which is seen operating on such occasions as Remembrance Day, both at local and national level, and at civic services with local authorities. It is also seen at religious services connected with the royal family. These are occasions when Church and State join in common religious expression and provide opportunities for communities to give vent to shared religious feelings. Civic religion becomes especially significant in times of war and can be expressed in hymns. 'O Valiant Hearts' was written in 1919 and points to how love of God and love of country were regarded as the same. The hymn speaks of the great sacrifice that many had made for their country and how this sacrifice can be compared with that made by Christ. The last verse reads:

> These were his servants, in his steps they trod,
> Following through death the martyred Son of God:
> Victor he rose; victorious too shall rise
> They who have drunk his cup of sacrifice.

2.28 The difficult and explosive potential of the encounter between civic religion and formal religion was well illustrated after the Falklands War in 1983 when the Prime Minister wanted a service highlighting a victory theme, whereas Church leaders wanted to commemorate the ending of a war in a more penitential atmosphere.

2.29 Expressions of implicit religion may occur spontaneously. For example, Edward Bailey has described the implicit religion of pubgoing.[18] The ritualised aspects of going to the pub at a certain time, meeting friends, sitting in a particular place, drinking from a 'special' glass, interacting with the group in the 'round' and with the people at the bar, may all work together to achieve an effect of well-being that is not entirely dependent on the consumption of alcohol. If any of the elements of the ritual are disturbed – a friend is ill, the seat is taken by an outsider – the effect can be to disrupt the whole evening.

2.30 Another example of the way implicit religion emerges spontaneously is seen in the way that flowers are laid at the site of a fatal accident or disaster. Such occasions encourage a certain level of debate about the sacred, evoking such comments as why should such accidents happen and how unfair it all appears. The offering of flowers sets up a temporary 'shrine' and the flowers express unspoken fears and prayers.

2.31 The public response to the Hillsborough disaster in Sheffield in 1989 when 94 Liverpool supporters died at the beginning of the semi-final of the FA Cup between Liverpool and Nottingham Forest reveals both the depth and extent of implicit religion and how it can interact creatively with formal religion. The disaster unfolded not only before the capacity crowd at the stadium, but also before the millions who were watching on television. In the days that followed one million people filed through Anfield, the home of the Liverpool Football Club, and the football pitch was hidden under a carpet of flowers, red and blue scarves and caps, mascots, souvenirs, football rattles and even a plaster Madonna from a Christmas crib. In an article in the *Independent*, Bishop David Sheppard and Archbishop Derek Worlock wrote: 'Blasphemy, unhealthy superstition, tawdry sentimentality. Or a rich blend of personal mourning, prayerful respect and genuine faith.'

2.32 When mourners attended the Liverpool cathedrals at this time, it was common to see football regalia there and in the moving memorial service which was broadcast on national television the Liverpool supporters' song, 'You'll never walk alone' was a significant part of the liturgy.[19]

2.33 An even more recent manifestation of implicit religion was in Dunblane in March 1996 when 16 infant school children and their teacher were shot during a class in the school gymnasium. This disaster not only shocked people in Britain, but also evoked messages of sympathy from around the world. Once again a mass of flowers was laid outside the school and the people of Dunblane filled their cathedral and local churches during the course of those disturbing days. Furthermore, the Prime Minister announced a national one minute's silence to remember the children and their teacher on the Sunday after the massacre. The observance of this silence appeared to be more widespread than the two minutes' silence traditionally observed on Remembrance Day. Candles were lit for the dead in Presbyterian churches where such a thing is not normally done. Furthermore, John Drane tells this story:

> I made my way to the school gates which had become a centre of devotion, transformed by the floral and other offerings placed there by residents and strangers alike. As I approached, the street outside the school was deserted apart from a handful of police officers, and a gang of youths aged, I suppose, about 17–20. As I watched, they took from their pockets sixteen nightlights – one for each dead child – and, kneeling on the damp pavement, arranged them in a circle, and then lit them – using glowing cigarettes to do so. They stood around the candles for a moment, then one of them said 'I suppose somebody should say something.' As they wondered how to do it, one of them spotted me, identified me as a minister, and called me over with the words, 'You'll know what to say.' Of course, the reality was quite different. As I stood there, tears streaming down my face, I had no idea what to say or how to say it. Words had not been especially useful to me, or anyone else, in this crisis. So we stood, holding on to one another for a moment, and then I said a brief prayer. That was the catalyst that enabled them too to start praying. A question came first: 'What kind of a world is this?' Another asked, 'Is there any hope?' Someone said, 'I wish I could trust God.' 'I'll need to change,' said a fourth one. As he did so, he looked first at me, and then glanced over his shoulder to the police who were on duty. He reached into his pocket and I could see he had a knife. He knelt again by the ring of candles, and quietly said 'I'll not be needing this now', as he tucked it away under some of the

flowers laying nearby. One of the others produced what looked like a piece of cycle chain, and did the same. We stood silently for a moment, and then went our separate ways.[20]

2.34 This moving story points up the symbiotic relation between the felt need of the improvised ritual and the minister of religion who supplies the right words to say. Out of this comes not only a release of prayer but also change and repentance as the young men lay down their weapons. When the full story of the nation's response to this event is documented in detail, the role of implicit religion, revealed in both its folk and civic forms, will be very apparent.

2.35 Apart from the rites of passage, Christmas and Harvest are times when the needs of implicit religion are explicitly met by celebrations within the Church. Many people who would not dream of darkening a church door are moved by their child's nativity play at school or will turn up for midnight mass and sit at the back. Similarly, Harvest Festival can still have a powerful impact even in the most urban areas, where the gifts might be tins of beans rather than garden fruit and vegetables but still drawing on the desire to give thanks and give back. So too the 'Churching of Women' in the Book of Common Prayer and its contemporary equivalent of 'Thanksgiving for the Birth of a Child' in *The Alternative Service Book* are rituals which meet deep pastoral needs recognised inside and outside the Church.

2.36 Implicit religion also finds expression in practices which, at first sight, seem totally divorced from any religion at all. For some, religious instincts find their outlets in the following of sport: the singing of hymns before rugby and football matches indicates the link with a religion; for others a regular ritual, such as the annual West Country carnivals, provides an expression for their religious instincts.

2.37 All religions, both formal and implicit, are prone to engender superstition, though superstition is a very subjective concept. Some Christians find genuflection before the Reserved Sacrament helpful to their devotion while others would regard both genuflection and the Reserved Sacrament as harmful superstitions. Some Christians use the veneration of relics to enrich their worship, while others would, again, dismiss this practice as harmful superstition. Superstition has negative overtones suggesting manipulation and magic, but perhaps it can best be defined as religious practice which may belittle humanity. Religion becomes superstition when it uses its rites and beliefs in an attempt to manipulate and control others, including God. Since superstitious behaviour underlies some forms of implicit religion, it is important for the Church to look at it carefully.

2.38 For some people, superstitious behaviour forms a kind of background, which is mostly unseen against the overlaid sophistication of modern life. However, it is surprising how many people touch wood or cross their fingers almost unconsciously. Superstitions about good and bad luck (black cats and horseshoes are lucky; walking under a ladder and opening an umbrella indoors are unlucky) hint at embryonic ritual actions for keeping oneself and one's family safe. Superstitious elements within rites of passage bring to the surface the human desire to influence the future by ensuring that all are safely gathered into the path of the good. For example: catching the bouquet at a wedding is lucky and presages marriage; wearing pearls at one's wedding leads to grief, hence *pearls are for tears ...*

2.39 Other superstitions are prejudicial: anyone who has seen *Mary Poppins* knows that chimney sweeps are lucky people to know; but some people who are genuinely black may suffer from a prejudicial and superstitious fear that is directed against them. Similarly, some negative attitudes to people with AIDS may arise from a superstitious fear of contact with an afflicted person, similar to fear of the 'evil eye' or 'witches' bane'. For example, in various *EastEnders* episodes in June/July 1996, a woman whose husband is HIV positive is prevented from approaching a new baby by members of the baby's family, who acknowledge their fear is unreasonable, but who are also unable to combat it. In some cultures, particular professions are anathematised. In the Dowayo culture in northern Cameroon, as described by the anthropologist Nigel Barley for example, blacksmiths cannot have any contact with ordinary people, because they are regarded as powerful and dangerous.[21] Rainmakers and witchdoctors may also fall into this category and their importance may be underestimated by Christians encountering the culture. In our own history, the wise woman has often turned into the witch, a person who becomes the agent of fear and object of reprisal.[22]

2.40 We can also see that a ritualised aspect of superstitious belief is characterised by some forms of magic. Some people may turn to spiritualism or some 'magic' practice such as astrology if they feel the Church has failed them, because here they obtain quickly what they need, at the expense of rational thought about what they are doing. Such people may also come back to the Church once their urgent need has passed. This is a challenge to the Church to identify and respond to such needs. For some people, the world becomes easily divided into angels and demons. In our own times, scapegoating remains an unpleasant but real social phenomenon: a person or group may become invested with whatever is superstitiously felt to be 'bad'. Consequently at Dunblane, the dead children were characterised as innocents and angels; the murderer, Thomas Hamilton, was characterised in the tabloid press as a demon: 'Monster burns in hell' was one front page headline when he was cremated.

2.41 We may say, then, that people who are searching for faith may try as hard as possible to eliminate the demons from their lives, and to relieve the anxiety of having to keep on the side of the angels. For some people, this results in creating their own liturgies and rituals which involve a destructive or cathartic element, such as when Christian survivors of sexual abuse burn photographs and weep openly together, but then:

> We returned for the Eucharist, lit candles for our loved ones or fellow survivors who could not come, received communion together and then sang of our strength, courage and survival. We ended with the hug of peace – embracing each other as sisters.[23]

2.42 For people who have been hurt or who are living in fear, the teaching of the Church about the reconciling work of God may come as a great relief. Jesus has a way of dealing with demons, which results in annihilation of the confusion and terror and restoration of confidence and right relations. As Christians, we have an opportunity to show that where the implicit religion of people results in despising and rejecting others, there is a model of justice, judgement, forgiveness and reconciliation in Christ which allows peace to replace fear and anger and recovery of those demonised, or anathematised (e.g. John 8.1–11). For Christ himself was a scapegoat and an outcast, like the vision of the Suffering Servant in Isaiah (Isaiah 53) whom God raised up (cf. Philippians 2.5–11).

The relationship between implicit religion and formal Christianity

2.43 The issue of the relationship between implicit or folk religion and formal Christianity is not a new one. Rather, there has always been an interplay between implicit religion and formal religion which can work in two directions. While implicit religion can borrow from formal Christianity (such as using the Bible as a fortune-telling device), formal religion can also borrow from implicit religion. A revealed religion, in particular, does not create its theology from nothing, but will borrow and incorporate other elements where God is seen to have brought about something new. We can see this in the Judeo-Christian tradition in the way that the faith in the God of Abraham, Isaac and Jacob related to local religions.

2.44 For example, in the first chapter of Genesis, the story of creation is a version of various creation myths current at the time. The Israelites who adapted the story changed some of the emphases to fit in with their understandings while allowing the implicit religion to remain. The story is therefore 'claimed' for the God of Israel, but the new story's challenge to the various myths does not remove the important sense-making elements of how human beings came to be. In the 'Enuma Elish', the Babylonian creation myth, for example, human beings are formed from the blood of a rebellious god and the purpose of humanity was to be at the service of the gods:

> Blood I will mass and cause bones to be. I will establish a savage, 'man' shall be his name. Verily, savage-man I will create. He shall be charged with the service of the gods that they might be at ease![24]

2.45 The writer of the Genesis account replaced this understanding of humanity by placing this part of God's creation as the culmination of the story and by making humanity, not as a slave, nor from the blood of a rebellious god, but in the image and likeness of God and the purpose of humanity was to be a steward of God's creation:

> So God created humankind in his image, in the image of God he created them; male and female he created them. God blessed them, and God said to them, 'Be fruitful and multiply and fill the earth and subdue it; and have dominion over the

The Search for Faith

fish of the sea and over the birds of the air and over every living thing that moves on the earth.' (Genesis 1.27–28)

2.46 This critical response to local religions and understandings is reflected throughout the Old Testament. Religious practices such as human sacrifice, magic and divination were strictly rejected, while others, such as altars, the offering of sacrifices, many birth, wedding and funeral customs were accepted and given new meanings. Similarly, in the New Testament Jesus accepts and adapts some popular religious practices such as anointing with saliva (cf. Mark 7.33; 8.23), healing by touch (e.g. Luke 8.44) and by the laying on of hands (e.g. Mark 8.11 and parallels), but he condemns magical approaches to power and refused to performs signs and wonders as ends in themselves (e.g. Matthew 12.39).

2.47 In his book *Europe: Was It Ever Really Christian?* Anton Wessels argues that Christianity takes root when it recognises and interacts with local religious practices. If the local folk religion is ignored or repressed, then not only will it reappear in a potentially dangerous form, but Christian influence is likely to be limited. Wessels uses the rise of National Socialism in the 1920s and 1930s in Germany to illustrate his thesis. He argues that National Socialism was a resurgence of a Teutonic paganism which has been repressed ('it had disappeared like the *Titanic*')[25] at the Christianisation of the Germans. Wessels uses a powerful quotation from Abraham Joshua Herschel:

> In its roots Nazism was a rebellion against the Bible, against the God of Abraham .... Sensing that it was Christianity that implanted the bond with the Hebrew Bible in the hearts of Westerners, Nazism resolved to exterminate both the Jews and Christianity and replace them with a revival of Teutonic paganism.[26]

2.48 What attitude does the Church adopt towards implicit religion? Does this attitude promote God's mission? There have been times when the Church has regarded implicit religion with disdain, rejecting it as pure superstition. This view has reflected a sense of social superiority of church attenders over and against the religiously disenfranchised lower classes. It was well exemplified over one hundred years ago by John Henry Newman:

> In the next place what has power to stir holy and refined souls is potent also with the multitude; and the religion of the multitude is ever vulgar and abnormal; it will ever be tinctured with fanaticism and superstition, while men are what they are. A people's religion is ever a corrupt religion, in spite of the provisions of Holy Church.[27]

2.49 However, there is strong evidence to suggest that what Newman calls 'fanaticism and superstition' but what we are calling implicit religion is not the preserve of one particular group of society: differences of social standing and education play no significant part.[28] One vicar recounts how the death of his predecessor was reported by a churchwarden, who was a retired naval officer, with the words, 'Fr X has now departed to rest with his forefathers', which reveals more about the cult of the dead and implicit religion than about traditional Christian theology. Thus, the Church needs to acknowledge that implicit religion is as much present inside the Church as outside, and the Church needs to relate to it appropriately. These elements of belief and practice may become noticeable in the most regular of church attenders at times of crisis. There is not a great chasm between orthodox Christian believers and implicit religion, indeed, there is no real gap between them, but they are integrally connected. As regular, religious practice diminishes so there is a drift away from Christian orthodoxies, and elements of implicit religion become more prominent.[29]

2.50 At the beginning of his book *Domination and the Arts of Resistance*, James C. Scott, Professor of Political Science at Yale University, quotes from Václav Havel:

> Society is a very mysterious animal with many faces and hidden potentialities, and ... it's extremely shortsighted to believe that the face society happens to be presenting to you at a given moment is its only true face. None of us knows all the potentialities that slumber in the spirit of the population.[30]

2.51 Scott then promotes an understanding of relationships which provides some insight into the relationship between implicit religion and formal Christianity. Scott uses the categories of the 'powerful' and the 'powerless' to show how the powerless can express their thoughts, concerns and resistance (their 'hidden transcript') in ingenious ways frequently not recognised by the powerful. Such expression can range from jokes against the powerful, to taking the opportunity to push them 'by accident' a little harder than usual. The Negro spirituals, composed and sung by the slaves on the plantations of America, were expressions of the hidden transcript of the powerless. Few plantation owners would have understood the political significance when they heard their slaves singing such biblically based songs as:

> When Israel was in Egypt's land
>
> Let my people go;
>
> Oppressed so hard they could not stand;
>
> Let my people go.

2.52 The agenda of the powerful is, in Scott's terminology, the 'public transcript', which represents the formal, acknowledged way in which the powerful relate to those in their power (the powerless). The crucial part of Scott's argument is that 'the public transcript, where it is not positively misleading, is unlikely to tell the whole story about power relations. It is frequently in the interest of both parties to tacitly conspire in misrepresentation', and he thereby points to the significance of the hidden transcript commenting, 'Unless one can penetrate the official transcript of both subordinates and elites, a reading of the social evidence will almost always represent a confirmation of the status quo in hegemonic terms.'[31]

2.53 Scott's arguments point to the significance of implicit religion, which can be described as the hidden transcript, if we seek a realistic picture of the context in which formal Christianity is functioning. Scott's approach indirectly raises important questions about power: can formal Christianity, a revealed religion with professional practitioners (that is, its ministers and administrators), be regarded as the 'powerful' with its 'public transcript'? Scott also provides a warning because if the hidden transcript of the 'powerless' is not allowed expression, then there is the potential for revolution. In other words, if formal Christianity does not allow the expression of implicit religion, there is the possibility that the latter will replace the former.

2.54 The Church needs to recognise and take implicit religion seriously and through the opportunities of contact, for example provided by the parochial system, to 'negotiate' with it. The rituals offered by the Church at the rites of passage and on other occasions will meet the needs of many outside the Church: it is surely important that the Church allows these needs to be met without placing insurmountable conditions on accessibility to these rituals which only allow a narrow interpretation of them? For example, a funeral in church or a marriage may be meeting a particular need for one group of people, but it may be meeting another need for another group. This privilege is to be a channel for God's grace and not to try and control or dictate the way in which God works. Such an understanding reflects the Church's role as a serving church.

Conclusions

2.55 The relationship between formal Christianity and implicit religion is not an area of concern confined only to Britain. Independent Churches have sprung up throughout the world, in particular in the developing countries of the Southern Hemisphere. Independent Churches have enshrined and made explicit beliefs and practices encountered in local cultures. One may therefore find a greater proportion of the worship taken up in singing, dancing, prophecy and healing. Furthermore, the growth of these churches is far outstripping that of the so-called mainstream churches. There is evidence that by the end of this century, there will be as many adherents of Indigenous Churches in Africa as there are Anglicans. Furthermore, and perhaps more disturbing, the Independent/mainstream Churches division reflects a First World/Third World division.[32] There can be little doubt that implicit religion is posing and will continue to pose one of the major challenges to the Church as it enters the twenty-first century.

2.56 There has been a tendency to dismiss implicit religion as folklore and superstition, regarding it as the religion of the uneducated. This attitude needs to be addressed seriously and urgently and this is being done vigorously and enthusiastically by the Network for the Study of Implicit Religion.[33] There are elements of implicit religion which are not compatible with the gospel of Jesus Christ just as there are some actions and practices legitimated by the Church which are not compatible with the gospel. These elements, such as using folk religion to control or invoke fear or to justify revenge, need to be vigorously challenged and resisted. Again, a 'test' question that can be asked is whether the practice or belief belittles or enhances humanity. Therefore a creatively critical response is required, which recognises the complicated interplay between a 'public' and a 'hidden' transcript and between what is life-enhancing and what is life-denying. It is, therefore, important that the Church listens (and *listening* is always the first step in any missionary endeavour) to God's voice in creation which includes the medium of implicit religion.

2.57 Acknowledging the significance of implicit religion should enable the Church to reflect upon the relationship between the active-believing minority and the less active-believing majority. The Church needs to find ways of reactivating religious language and concepts which may be buried in expressions of implicit religion. Christians could also spend more time working on how to build bridges to people's rite-making and personal 'sacraments'. This reflection would enable the local churches to be in touch with the deepest hopes and fears of their communities and provide appropriate symbols and images in order that the communication of the gospel may be more effective.

2.58 The Church is already taking advantage of a number of opportunities to communicate the gospel where implicit religion becomes explicit in rites of passage such as baptism, marriage, and funerals, or in festivals such as Christmas, Harvest and various civic services including Remembrance Sunday. It is important that pastoral strategies enable these missionary opportunities to be used to the full. There are many different ways of viewing these occasions. The Church should not misuse its position to limit or control the activity of God.

2.59 Furthermore, local churches are in a position to develop appropriate liturgies for their communities which will enable implicit religion to become explicit. Examples of such occasions could be a celebration of All Souls, to which the relatives of all who have died in the parish over the previous year can be invited and the practice of house blessings. The idea of home liturgy could also be extended.

2.60 Mission and ministry are integrally connected. The ministry that the Church offers comes from a missionary strategy, which will be implicit even if it is not made explicit. Because the Church has access to a large part of the community, not least through the parish system, its ministers and representatives need to use this privilege with respect and care, not inflicting the

Church but offering the Church, showing that they respect and take seriously those whom they meet. A creative and open pastoral approach will enable implicit religion to become explicit.

2.61 Finally, it is worth remembering that church attenders are as much part of the world as non-church attenders and so church attenders are also open to the beliefs and practices of implicit religion. As the Church focuses on the relationship with implicit religion, it is at the same time focusing on activities and beliefs deep within itself.

Summary

KEY WORDS

- implicit religion ● folk religion ● civic religion ● rituals
- superstition ● restricted code ● hidden transcript

The high level of general belief among those who are not committed to a faith tradition can be expressed as implicit religion. Such a religious consciousness, which is exemplified in the language we use and in the ideas and concepts we have inherited from our culture may come to the surface spontaneously, particularly during life crises or times of national crisis or tragedy.

Implicit religion exists alongside formal religion and the two may interact. If the Church cannot meet the felt needs of some people, the strength of their implicit religion may drive them to satisfy their needs elsewhere.

People need rituals in their lives, but we live in a society where many occasions for ritual have been eroded. Consequently, people feel a strong lack of this opportunity for expressing themselves and may make up their own rituals. Baptisms, marriages and funerals may therefore become critical occasions when the Church has a great opportunity to reach people in their needs.

Superstition may show how people desire strongly to ward off evil and keep on the side of the good. Equally, they may become trapped by it, or demonise people or things they designate as bad. The Church has a strong message to give here, for the gospel promises freedom from fear and overwhelming anxiety. Further, the example of Jesus's own attitude and dealings with the outcast, the demonised, the sick and the tortured, gives Christians a model of how God's healing and recovery can come into damaged lives.

Civic religion also creates an opportunity for the Church and implicit religion to meet and interact positively. In times of national mourning, for example, people's mostly unarticulated belief may become more overt and they will look to the Church for ways in which to express it.

The historical relation between formal faith and implicit religion even from Old Testament times shows that formal faith is able to reject or absorb elements of implicit religion. Further, implicit religion can flourish even within the Church itself. There are no hard and fast boundaries, but the Church cannot afford to ignore the effects of implicit religion, either within formal Christianity, or outside.

Another way of looking at implicit religion is in terms of the 'hidden transcript' of the powerless against the 'official transcript' of the powerful. If the 'hidden transcript' is not allowed expression, then revolution may occur. This means the Church must take implicit religion seriously.

Further reading

Bailey, Edward (ed.), *A Workbook in Popular Religion*, Partners Publications, 1986.

Bruce, Steve, *Religion in Modern Britain*, OUP, 1995.

Thomas, Keith, *Religion and the Decline of Magic*, Peregrine edition, Penguin Books, 1978.

Wessels, Anton, *Europe: Was It Ever Really Christian?* SCM, 1994.

Interested readers might also contact:

The Network for the Study of Implicit Religion
Winterbourne Rectory
Bristol
BS17 1JQ

CONTACT MAKERS

Packs of ideas for contacting people at baptisms, weddings and funerals available from:

Mrs Claire Hams
Board of Mission
Church House
Great Smith Street
London
SW1P 3NZ

HOME LITURGIES

Contact

Marjorie Allen
Diocesan Church House
175 Harborne Park Road
Harborne
Birmingham
B17 0BH

Things to do

- **AIM:** to see where your church or group meets the needs of implicit religion and see where it operates in your Christian community.
- **PURPOSE:** to create mission opportunities for the Christian community to interact with people's implicit religion.

BIBLE VERSE

He [Jesus] took the blind man by the hand and led him out of the village: and when he had put saliva on his eyes, and laid his hands on him, he asked him 'Can you see anything?' (Mark 8.23)

Things to do include:
a. Listing superstitions
b. Looking at hymns
c. Describing secular rituals
d. Discussion starters

1. SUPERSTITIONS

Get people to make a list of superstitious beliefs, or ask people in pairs to look at superstitions in categories such as marriage, death, good luck, bad luck. You might be able to use good luck cards or messages from the local paper.

Ask people in pairs to talk about which superstitions they observe (even if not very seriously) and ask them to think about why they do so. Ask pairs to think about how far implicit religion influences their lives.

Ask people in pairs to think about what superstitious beliefs people might have about church, about the minister, about church furnishings, about graveyards, etc. You might also use a film clip of a horror film that includes churches, graveyards, crucifixes, etc.

2. HYMNS

Have a look through your hymn book and see if you can find examples of implicit religion in some of the well-known hymns. Or have a look at spirituals. (Someone might like to play or sing some of the hymns or spirituals.)

3. RITUALS

In groups of four or five, ask people to identify rituals outside the church, such as pubgoing. Ask them to write down what the elements of the ritual are.

Ask the whole group to discuss what secular rituals they are involved in. What, if anything, makes church rituals different or special?

Pool all these ideas by drawing up a list of ways in which your own implicit religion can build bridges to those who are searching for faith.

4. DISCUSSION STARTERS

a. Is people's implicit religion helpful or harmful to the Church?

b. Does the Church use its power to suppress people's implicit religion unhelpfully?

c. How do you think services in your church or group meet the needs of implicit religion?

d. Do you think there are ways in which worship, prayer, Bible study, youth groups, etc. could appeal to those searching for faith? If so, how?

e. How should Christians treat people who are either helped or trapped by superstition?

f. Do you think your Christian community fails to take implicit religion seriously?

g. How can your church or group be involved in civic religion? Does this mean taking more initiatives?

Notes

1. Church attendance figures (published in P. Brierley and V. Hiscock (eds), *UK Christian Handbook*, CRA, 1993) are 14.4 per cent for 1992 and are estimated at 13.9 per cent for 1995.
2. Although these figures give a general impression of the state of belief, their precision cannot be guaranteed; a similar survey of a London Borough in the 1940s (see Mass Observation, *Puzzled People*, Gollancz, 1948, p.32) noted: 'Of the doubters, agnostics and atheists ... over a quarter say they pray on occasions to the God whose existence they doubt.' To keep these figures in perspective, post-war surveys point to an increase in unbelief. For further details and analysis of these statistics see Steve Bruce, *Religion in Modern Britain*, Oxford University Press, 1995, from which these statistics have been quoted.
3. See David Hay, 'Individuals' Religious Experiences' in Edward Bailey (ed.), *A Workbook in Popular Religion*, Partners Publications, 1986, p.12.
4. See P. Hiebert, 'Popular Religion', in J. M. Phillips and R. T. Coote (eds), *Toward the Twenty-First Century in Christian Mission*, Eerdmans, 1993, p.255.
5. C. Geertz, *Local Knowledge: Further Essays in Interpretive Anthropology*, Basic Books, 1985, referred to in Hiebert, ibid., p.255.

6. 'Religious Development and Ritual' in James Fowler, Karl Ernst Nipkow and Friedrich Schweitzer, *Stages of Faith and Religious Development: Implications for Church, Education and Society*, SCM, 1992, p.200.
7. Madeleine Bunting, 'Lost in these trivial pursuits', the *Guardian*, 24 February 1996.
8. J. C. Frazer, *The Golden Bough: A Study in Magic and Religion*, Papermac edition, 1987, p.126.
9. There is now an increased interest in 'green cemeteries' and in planting trees to commemorate the dead.
10. M. Eliade, *Images and Symbols*, Harper Torchbooks, 1961, pp.160–61.
11. See David Jones, *Anathemata*, Faber, 1952.
12. Edward Bailey, in *Country Way*, Issue 7, Autumn 1994, p.19.
13. *EastEnders*, 16 October 1995.
14. Philip Larkin, 'Church Going' in *Collected Poems*, Faber, 1988, pp.97–8; 'Aubade', pp.208–9; 'An Arundel Tomb', pp.110–11.
15. François Kabasele, 'Christ as Ancestor and Elder Brother' in Robert J. Schreiter (ed.), *Faces of Jesus in Africa*, SCM, 1992, p.119.
16. For example, see Marjorie Allen's Home Liturgies selection, Diocesan Office, 175 Harborne Park Road, Harborne, Birmingham B17 0BH.
17. See Anton Wessels, *Europe: Was It Ever Really Christian?* SCM, 1994.
18. Edward Bailey, '"Implicit Religion?" A Follow-up to David Martin', *Crucible*, Jan–Mar 1995, pp.19–25.
19. For further discussion, including details of the *Independent* quotation, see G. Davie, *Religion in Britain since 1945: Believing without Belonging*, in the *Making Contempory Britain* series, Blackwell, 1994, pp.88ff.
20. John Drane, 'Dunblane: A Personal Testimony'.
21. See Nigel Barley, *The Innocent Anthropologist*, Penguin, 1983 and *A Plague of Caterpillars*, Penguin, 1986.
22. For a comprehensive study of the relationships between formal religion and implicit religion, including wise women and witches, see Keith Thomas, *Religion and the Decline of Magic*, Peregrine edition, 1978.
23. From a report of the Christian Survivors of Sexual Abuse (CSSA) retreat, October 1994, an ecumenical weekend in Crewe led by a religious sister and survivor. The liturgy was led by an Anglican female priest survivor.
24. Tablet VI, l.5–9.
25. A. Wessels, op. cit., p.164.
26. H. Kasimov and B. L. Sherwin (eds), *No Religion is an Island: Abraham Joshua Herschel and Interreligious Dialogue*, 1991, p.4, quoted in Wessels, op. cit., p.163.
27. J. H. Newman, *Certain Difficulties Felt By Anglicans in Catholic Teaching*, Longmans, Green & Co., 1888, pp.80–81.
28. See P. Brown, *The Cult of the Saints*, University of Chicago Press, 1981, p.19.

29. See G. Davie, op. cit., p.76.
30. James C. Scott, *Domination and the Arts of Resistance*, Yale University Press, 1990, p.90.
31. Ibid., pp.2, 90.
32. See Walter Hollenweger, 'After Twenty Years' Research in Pentecostalism', *Theology* LXXXVII, November 1984, 403–12.
33. This is based at Winterbourne Rectory, Bristol BS17 1JQ under the direction of Canon Dr Edward Bailey.

3

The world is my oyster

My name's Adam. I think it's up to me to decide what's right – work it out for myself. I know there's God, but it's God getting through to me, not driving me to join up to some organisation. I believe in lots of things, karma and reincarnation and that. It makes sense when you look at it, right?

I'm really worried about what we're doing to the world and how we're destroying it. I think the earth talks to us and that the earth is full of power. I've done cards, pyramids, stones – and all that turns out pretty hopeful for me. I like to glimpse the future. I feel like I'm in control of my destiny. I like to work out, too, to feel good, really alive, right? Then I'll have a good massage to chill out, let myself go. Or meditate, be quiet. Then I know it's God telling me it's OK, it really is.

I don't need Church. You have to believe the party line, but I've worked all this out for myself. I want to pray and worship what I want in my own way and the Church doesn't give me that.

Introduction

We do not live in a godless or totally secularised society. We live in a pluralist society in which most of the world's faiths are represented. Also, many people outside formal religion feel that their life has been touched by the transcendent and seek to respond to this. Such responses, however, are often conditioned by the kind of culture in which we now live. The highly privatised culture and the proliferation of choice inspire many people to make their spiritual journeys through a pick'n'mix approach. Such people may be attracted by New Age practices, or adopt a spirituality focused on the natural world.

In a stressful world, self-esteem and self-worth may become the driving factors in developing spirituality, and these may be allied to a need to feel good about one's bodily health, appearance and sexuality.

The challenge to the Church is to recognise the profile of this kind of burgeoning spirituality and to show how Christianity can meet its needs. Christianity should not have to ride roughshod over expressions of contemporary spirituality, for there is a capacity for a dynamic and interactive relationship between the two. Christian faith has resources in its traditions, such as Celtic spirituality, which can speak to the needs of those who are searching for faith. Christians also have the opportunity to build bridges in mission to those whose idea of God is as yet undeveloped, but whose desires are for blessing, wholeness and hope. Christian people have Jesus Christ to offer as a pattern of human existence, and the witness of the Christian community to offer as a way of human living. The perfection of these in the kingdom can be held out to those who are struggling to live in the complexity of the present as a perfect hope and proper end for our spiritual journeys.

How contemporary spirituality challenges the Church

There was also commonly expressed, if often only indirectly articulated, the feeling that (churchgoing) was not all that 'being religious' really consisted of.[1]

3.1. We have noted, in both previous chapters, that the level of generalised belief remains high. In the chapter on implicit religion we recognised the deep down residues of belief. Now we need to move on to discover *what* it is that people outside the mainstream religions believe, in order to see how this does or does not interact with the Church's mission to proclaim the Good News of Jesus Christ.

3.2 The research undertaken by the Alister Hardy Research Centre provides us with information about various forms of generalised belief. If we look at examples from some of this research, we can begin to see trends which fit in with what we have observed in earlier chapters. In the examples which follow, it should be remembered that they are drawn from a specific sample of *young* people, who are at a particular stage in the search for faith and who are able to tell their story.

Examples

A. Sometimes, I don't know when but I sort of fall into my own little world, where my mind just wanders through things and then sorts it out. It is hard to explain. I am really sitting apart from the world, and it just gives me a sensation; it is as if my inner self is healing me and giving me a new perspective. I don't know, I can't explain it, you have to experience it for yourself; may be it's God or part of God in me, just as it is in everyone else, but you have to find it.

B. We have to believe in something, otherwise life is terribly pointless. That's why people believe in a God or a religion. There must be a God or something behind it all, but I think that it is too exceptional and almighty for our petty minds to interpret. People who are really into religion are for ever looking for this thing. But they never find it. I believe life is our God. We can either make our life a good one and one to remember, or we can be evil. It is totally up to us, no one else can decide this for us. I believe I was put here for a purpose, but I think I have done it all wrong.

C. Sometimes when nothing really exciting is happening in my life, but at the time I am not unhappy, a great relaxing, motivating feeling grips me. I feel excited about something, and know a good thing is going to happen. To me, it feels as if something is governing my life, balancing out good and bad experiences. Although I have been brought up without religion, and am unsure about the existence of God, I can't help wondering if this could possibly be God in action. Very frequently I debate this issue within myself, trying to reason these feelings out.[2]

D. Often when I am walking outside, sometimes when I am somewhere I have been many times before, or somewhere new, I feel a sort of softening feeling that blends me as an individual into everything else. It is like being sucked into an enormous void – only it's full of unimportant things which make up a whole. I notice things, little things that I couldn't have cared about before but now seem wonderful.[3]

E. Sometimes I sit in a dark room, like my bedroom, and feel a power around me. I don't think of bad things that have happened but I only think about how lucky I am to be alive on this beautiful earth. Everything else is unimportant. I can get this feeling on my own.[4]

3.3 What is interesting about these examples, is the high degree of personal and individual language: 'my own little world' (A), 'I believe I was put here for a purpose' (B), 'I debate this issue within myself' (C), 'blends me as an individual into everything else' (D), 'I can get this feeling on my own' (E).

3.4 In view of what we have seen previously in the chapter on belonging about individualisation and post-materialism, it is entirely consistent that this kind of religious experience should be couched in terms of the individual, alone and isolated, trying to make sense of an understanding of the 'other', of some vague transcendence.[5] In these examples, the experiences are isolating and isolative, rather than in any sense being community-building or corporate. Is it so strange, then, that the people who have these experiences have difficulties in locating their search for faith within a corporate body, the Church, which offers religious experience in solidarity with other believing Christians? The former Archbishop of York, Dr John Habgood, makes this point when he says, 'I think the whole post-modernist tendency towards individualism makes it very difficult to believe or to find where a faith which has universal claims fits into an individualist approach to life.'[6] How does the Church reach out to the many people having these kinds of experiences in a way that allows these experiences to become part of legitimate faith development? This question is especially pertinent when we consider the power and intensity of these experiences, for is it perhaps a quality of the power and intensity that the experience is personal and unconnected to anyone else?

3.5 In the first place, we should perhaps learn to value the way people are able to articulate powerful experiences of the 'other' or of the numinous. It is clear that experiences of this kind are widespread, but for some people it is simply not possible to articulate them. Where there are no words, the experience is untransmissible, unsharable; the sense of God's presence is powerful but silent, so private as to be untouchable. Perhaps, then, we should begin by assuming that all human beings are touched by God in some way during their lives, but this activity of the missionary God is ultimately personal and unarticulated. If this is true, then the mission of the Church does not start from nothing in its outreach, but approaches each person as a place where God has already been. Further, as the Church seeks to proclaim, it speaks into ground which has already been seeded by the Spirit and it should not seek to till that ground again. The assumption that God is ever at work in the world and that we should seek to discover what God has already done and work with this under the guidance of the Holy Spirit,[7] is a theological stance which is now increasingly important for mission.

3.6 If the Church is going to engage with contemporary spirituality, then it has to deal with the various elements of that spirituality and use these to help people test their emergent spiritual experiences inside Christianity. For this reason, we now need to look at some of the component elements of contemporary spirituality and see which are open to Christian relationship and encounter.

Being in control

3.7 These examples given above point up how religious experience can be related to a sense of purpose, but the purpose is itself related to the affirmation of self-worth and to the ability to control: 'as if my inner self is healing me and giving me a new perspective' (A), 'it is totally up to us' (B). The sense that there is a power inside or outside the self which can be accessed by the self is a positive and healing experience leading to joy and hopefulness. This can be located and named as God: 'maybe it's God or part of God in me' (A), 'there must be a God or something behind it all ... I believe life is our God' (B), 'I can't help wondering if this could possibly be God in action' (C).

3.8 Where this happens, such experiences do not seem far from specifically Christian understandings. For example:

> Often too I feel a presence with me, it can comfort me when I am worried about something or when things seem to be going right for me, it seems to fill me with an amazing sense of happiness, completeness and knowledge that everything is somehow in control. Being a Christian I would call this God.[8]

3.9 In some cases, reliance on 'other Power' can seem to belittle the self and the power of the self to be in control:

> I feel that turning to outside influence is a total denial of self-capability
>
> I usually say what the hell
>
> I stand on my own feet. I have no God, only hope.[9]

3.10   In these examples, it is clear that any sense of dependency on God's power affects the sense of self-worth and is therefore to be rejected. The Church's understanding here might be that God affirms human personhood and that the sense of self-worth is itself a religious experience. It is not necessary to renounce the strength of the self in order to come to Christian faith, but to understand that Jesus releases us into a way of being human which permits the exploration of our full human potential. Consequently, there may well be further discoveries in subsequent communion with God, including a self-giving which will lead to greater self-worth and discovery of new strength.

Feeling good

3.11   Another theme emerging from this kind of example is the need to feel good about oneself. The need is also connected with self-worth and value and with the desire to have and maintain control: 'as if my inner self is healing me' (A), 'a great relaxing, motivating feeling grips me. I feel excited about something, and know a good thing is going to happen' (C), 'softening feeling ... I notice things that ... now seem wonderful' (D), 'I ... feel a power around me ... how lucky I am to be alive' (E).

3.12   Or, as W. B. Yeats writes in 'Vacillation',

> While on the shop and street I gazed
> My body on a sudden blazed;
> And twenty minutes more or less
> It seemed, so great my happiness
> that I was blessed and could bless.[10]

3.13   When we look at this kind of language, we move on to an area that is increasingly important in an understanding of contemporary spirituality, which is the need for people to feel good about the human body and to acquire feelings of peace and harmony within the life environment. This is entirely in accord with a post-materialist society, with its emphasis on quality of life, and as such may be a good indicator of the feelings of those who are most integrated into western culture. In this sense the Church meets a challenge, because while reaching into the kind of spirituality that demands self-fulfilment and self-realisation, the Church still has to maintain its option for, and solidarity with, the poor. The Church is committed to those who may be spiritually mature but still dealing with material needs and who have a long way to go before they can encounter the post-material situation. The Church is therefore faced with this question: when the needs of the poor are met, is this emphasis on feeling good what we most want to offer, or is it rather that the Church should in all humility take the opportunity to learn from the spirituality of the poor? The largest version of this question is a political one, but the Church must also address the matter of spiritual growth. Christians cannot ignore the way loss of self-esteem and feelings of worthlessness can destroy a person, but the restoration of self-worth that is offered in Jesus Christ is not power over others, or increased or privileged status, but confidence that the self is uniquely loved. This may be a touchstone of difference between contemporary spirituality outside the mainstream religions and the life in Christ offered by the Church.

3.14 The way in which the 'feel-good factor' operates in the public sphere and in the commodity market is evident in the number of 'alternative' or 'New Age' therapies and practices which are currently around. Some of these are in the business of healing, with emphasis on the relief of pain and developing a more positive approach to life. Some concentrate on the idea that a healthy body is directly related to peace of mind and to a spiritual wholeness. Consequently, it is possible to obtain a number of 'therapies' in various ways according to one's inclination and one's pocket. At the bottom of the pile, as it were, are such practices as aromatherapy, which in the Boots and Body Shop versions may be little more than fragrant bath oil or perfumes, albeit often preferentially drawn from natural sources rather than artificially produced. Some of these are sold as massage oils, with the indication that pleasure and calm are to be derived from scent and tactile contact.

3.15 Other therapies involve consultations with people qualified in various forms of massage: reflexology, palpation of the foot, is one such currently in vogue. Other forms of massage practice may also be advertised in the local paper, but while some relate to particular needs, such as pregnancy and back problems, they can be mixed with advertisements for a much commoner form of physical service. The practice of colonic irrigation is also supposed to cleanse and purify the body from the inside out. Some of these body-centred experiences create intense feelings of well-being, which, when the effect wears off, can be repeated as necessary. The only cost may be money. When the novelty of one therapy wears off, another takes its place. In an age when the message about the danger of drug use is heard more clearly, the 'trip' or 'fix' can now be through the 'body spiritual' rather than by direct action of chemicals on physiological processes. Another implication is that the stress of modern living interferes with a person's spiritual well-being, which has to be restored by removing the stress. This highlights

Figure 5 Feeling good?

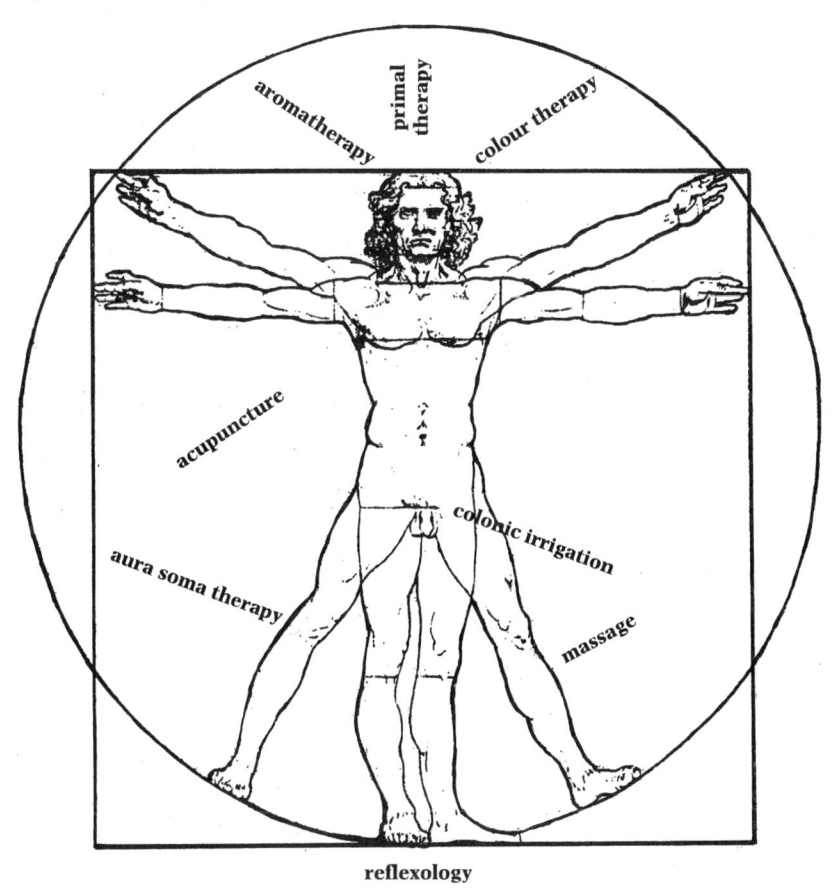

the fact that for many people in contemporary western society, life is indeed very stressful and the need for stress management has to be recognised by the Church, where Jesus's words 'Come to me all you that are weary and are carrying heavy burdens, and I will give you rest' (Matthew 11.28) may come to have new significance. On the other hand, it may become a barrier to Christian commitment if joining a church is seen to be adding to a person's stress in relation to their family, job, or the church's own expectations.

3.16 What has the Church to say to people whose spiritual life is nurtured in this way? First, there is no point throwing out the baby with the perfumed bath water. Many of these therapies and practices are vestigial or adapted versions of old religious practices, while yoga and the chanting of mantras have a well-validated place in eastern religions, and indeed, awareness of eastern religions may have much to do with the adoption of some practices. Meditation, fasting and prayer also have honourable traditions in Christianity. We should also mention that stimulation of the senses, including the use of scent, is part of authentic Christian tradition. We may say, however, that in New Age and other practices, such as colour therapy, aromatherapy, meditation music, etc., the focus is often missing. Instead of using these techniques as a means to an end – to obtain a closer relationship with God – these practices are seen as an end in themselves: a feeling of value and enrichment, without meaning. The powerful stimulation of the senses which is unified in, for example, Orthodox worship, is fragmented in these New Age practices. The reaction of some Christians has been to condemn these kinds of practices and therapies, especially where these appear as a hedonistic or self-indulgent retreat from the world, while others have tried to reach into them. So the St Marylebone Centre for Healing and Counselling provides both complementary medicine, through its NHS practice, and spiritual direction.

3.17 Is it possible, however, to see a kind of scale in which at one end is someone adding aromatherapy oil to bath water, and at the other end the use of practices for a specific religious end, such as druidism or wicca? If so, when does it become necessary to define criteria that distinguish one from the other? At what point in the scale does the label 'incompatible with Christianity' apply? A number of cases in which some members of churches have been revealed as being simultaneously practitioners of other forms of spirituality or religious practice have caused problems for ministers and congregations, and some such people have been simply asked to leave. Here, looking at the mission implications, we might say that the response to such a person depends on the amount of distraction from the Christian occupation of working for and in God's kingdom is created by that person's choices. At the same time, the appropriate response is surely not a knee-jerk defensive reaction, but a loving concern undergirded by confidence in the truth of the Christian message. Further, mission may not mean trying to dissuade a person from a particular practice (unless this is causing real mental or physical harm), but encouraging him or her to work through it and beyond it into an understanding that a deeper and more long-lasting satisfaction can be found in what is offered by the Christ-like God.

3.18 It is also worth noting that an increasing number of churches now hold healing services, or may incorporate a time of healing ministry and prayer within the traditional liturgies. It is also characteristic of such ministry times that they may include a defined tactile experience: the laying on of hands with prayer, or anointing with oil. It may be that the sensitive development of such ministries within the body of the Church's worship may serve to attract those who need to have their bodies affirmed and cherished under God and who have perhaps grown past self-centred practices which are not directly referential of God.

3.19 Here we cannot avoid addressing the abuse of power which can go on even within the Church. People who surrender themselves to the care of others may leave themselves open to exploitation; unscrupulous practitioners have opportunities to make money from those who need help but cannot really afford expensive therapies, or may in extreme cases abuse people's bodies. Uncontrolled situations may also leave practitioners open to blame and accusation from those they have tried to help. For this reason, the St Marylebone Centre has a Code of Ethics and Practice. There are no rooms without visual access from the corridors and healing by touching the affected part of the body does not take place. This enables the Centre to provide services for cases of need within proper guidelines and boundaries. This protection of people and practitioners also needs to be taken seriously by the whole Church.

3.20 Unless the Church is seen to be offering such people something they want and need, however, it is likely that those growing up with 'pick'n'mix' practices will simply seek more and more complex versions of the same thing without even finding a place to locate the spiritual part of these experiences. The lesson for the Church here is that it can no longer be afraid of the notion of embodiment, for human beings are created corporeal and sexual. Mission has to reach out and nurture holistically, not just in terms of intellectual apologetics. In this respect the Church has to be more aware of people's feelings about their bodies and to deal genuinely with issues concerning our creatureliness and sexuality.[11]

3.21 The fact that many people do need to feel good about their bodies also challenges the Church to *affirm* our creatureliness, as beings made in God's image and this includes our sexual nature. In a highly individualised society, relationships, including intimate relationships, may be less easily entered into and sustained, leading to casual and impersonal encounters. People may draw the boundaries of their individual needs so tightly around themselves that it becomes almost impossible to let another person in, to communicate with them openly and honestly, and to give of oneself in sharing and mutuality. The search for love, like the search for faith, can be characterised by frustration and loneliness. Christians then may be challenged by the fact that an ideal of lifelong faithful commitment may be for many in modern society a remote concept or impossible dream, yet it is part of our task to show forth a model of enduring and unchanging love. We are challenged to witness to a relationship with God which makes it possible for us to be faithful and committed in the giving of our hearts, minds and bodies to another person, as to God. Further, the recovery and affirmation of concepts such as faithfulness, self-giving, obedience and forgiveness, in respect of all our relationships, including our sexual relationships, are an important mission task in a world of emphasis on self and personal choice. Christians have to deal with a society in which Aldous Huxley's satirical words 'ending is better than mending' have real force.[12]

The future and hope

> Hey you, you're a child in my head
> you haven't walked yet
> your first words have yet to be said
> But I swear you'll be blessed ...

> ... you'll be blessed
> you'll have the best
> I promise you that
> I'll pick a star from the sky
> pull your name from a hat
> I promise you that you'll be blessed
>
> (Elton John, 'Blessed' from *Made in England*, 1995,
> William A. Bong Ltd, Mercury Records)

3.22 Another important theme of contemporary spirituality is a need to look forward to the future and to hope. The current popularity of psychic fairs indicates increasing interest in fortune-telling and reading the future. New Age practices have many ways of doing this, from sophisticated versions of looking at your stars in the daily paper, to consulting crystals, the Tarot, other forms of modern divination and even Mystic Meg, a television personality who predicts for you if you are the kind of person who is going to be several million pounds richer by the end of the Saturday lottery draw. While it is easy to laugh at Mystic Meg, it is not so easy to laugh at the reports that wives of recent presidents of the United States consult fortune-tellers and astrologers. This story illustrates how people may fasten their hopes and affections on those who can supposedly help them to face the future.

> The death of Patric Walker last week knocked a nation for six. As one letter said: 'I couldn't help but shed a tear when I heard of Patric Walker's death. In a way he was like one of my relatives, even closer. He was a leading light in my small world. He used to tell of me, touch my life, push me towards creating a better tomorrow.'[13]

3.23 The desire to know the future before it happens and the need for messages from the transcendental realm have a long history. In the Old Testament, casting lots (see e.g. 1 Samuel 14.41–42) and consultation of the Urim and Thummim (see Exodus 28.30; Deuteronomy 33.8; 1 Samuel 28.6) precede verbal prophecy and symbolic actions. What seems to have been lost from today's practices is the sense that we are moving into *God's* future. As Christians, we believe that the future is not unsure or uncertain, but already achieved for us. All we have to do is work to bring ourselves and our fellow people into the vision set out for us in Scripture and in the tradition of the Church. New Agers reject this vision, believing that this belongs to the Age of Pisces which is passing, and are left with the Age of Aquarius in which human consciousness becomes ever more perfect. In this sense followers of New Age see the Christ-like God as being of the past and not of the future and have turned away from the reality of God's promise and find themselves trying to make sense of a world without a coherent and meaningful vision of the future. For them, then, making sense of the chaotic must come through the power of the human person and our resourcefulness in 'pick'n'mix' to make a whole. This is a condition of what is called post-modernity and leads some to believe that we are now in a post-Christian culture.

3.24 However, for many, an encounter with the Christian vision of God's kingdom made real on earth and the *eschaton* in which all things are created new and perfect, is not seen as a living reality. For such people sometimes, our Christian hope is dismissed as dead and dust even before they have had the chance to encounter it. The challenge to the Church is to present the vision of God's future as the sustaining vision of authentic spirituality, into which all desires to know what is in store may be poured and satisfied with God's promises.

> Encumbered forever by desire and ambition
> There's a hunger still unsatisfied
> Our weary eyes still stray to the horizon
> Though down this road we've been so many times
>
> The grass was greener
> The light was brighter
> The taste was sweeter
> The nights of wonder
> With friends surrounded
> The dawn mist glowing
> The water flowing
> The endless river
>
> Forever and ever
>
> (Pink Floyd, 'High Hopes' from *The Division Bell*, 1994, Pink Floyd Music, EMI Records)

3.25 This song, which refers not only to the stress of life, but also to the desire for quality and permanence, opens and closes with the persistent ringing of a (church?) bell, the 'division bell'. Those on the outside are aware of their unsatisfied hunger. The challenge to Christians is to convince those who hear the bell that it is not the death knell of Christianity but that there is a hope of a future that is indeed sweeter and brighter, and one which lasts 'forever and ever'.

The natural world

3.26 Another important aspect of contemporary spirituality is the increased emphasis on the numinous aspects of the natural world and feelings of interconnectedness with all of creation, without losing the sense of the supremacy of self. This manifests itself in places of pilgrimage, such as Glastonbury, an interest in ley lines and in the planet as a self-regulating being: Gaia.[14] Where people's spirituality is inclined in this direction, green issues come to the fore and ecology and spirituality become mixed. Non-exploitation of the environment is stressed and non-harming of living beings. 'Do what you like but harm none' is the ethical maxim of some groups, including paganism. This touches the Church's pursuit of justice, peace and the integrity of creation in its task of furthering God's kingdom on earth. However, it also reinforces the challenge to the Church to be clear about its moral teaching and commitments in a world in which ethical issues become ever more complex. The Church also has to be clear about the relation between God and creation. The pantheistic colouring of some New Age beliefs may be attractive to many who are searching for faith, but Christianity sees a dynamic relation between the creator God and the created order. This allows us to perceive more of God as the creator and sustainer of all that is (see Chapter 4) by finding analogy rather than identity in the natural world.

3.27 For example, the seventeenth-century poet Andrew Marvell writes about a drop of dew as if it were longing for the sun to draw it back towards the sky. By using the analogy of the morning dew's evaporation in the sunlight, he writes about the dew as if it were a soul longing to be reunited with God.[15] Moreover, many other Christians have found God in contemplation of the natural world and have been able to express this. For example:

The Search for Faith

> There are nights that are so still
> that I can hear the small owl calling
> far off and a fox barking
> miles away. It is then that I lie
> in the lean hours awake listening
> to the swell born somewhere in the Atlantic
> rising and falling, rising and falling
> wave on wave on the long shore
> by the village, that is without light
> and companionless. And the thought comes
> of that other being who is awake, too,
> letting our prayers break on him,
> not like this for a few hours,
> but for days, years, for eternity.[16]

3.28 Some argue that contemporary interest in the numinous power of nature taps into a spirituality that is more feminine, such that 'Mother Earth' corrects the overweening power of the traditional father-sky-god. The challenge to the Church here is that it has chosen from almost its earliest times to cause a patriarchal, austere version of Christianity to dominate and has written its theology to reinforce and sustain it. Today, there are seen various reactions to this. One such reaction occurs at the level of language, where it is felt that calling attention to the male, dominating language of Christian theology and worship, raises consciousness about what is missing and may seek to replace it. For example:

> God our mother,
> you hold our life within you;
> nourish us at your breast,
> and teach us to walk alone.
> Help us so to receive your tenderness
> and respond to your challenge
> that others may draw life from us
> in your name. Amen.[17]

3.29 Others have pointed out that it is not necessary radically to overturn traditional Christian imagery about the fatherhood of God, because there is already a tradition of use of female images and expression in the Church which can be rediscovered. For example, in Isaiah the Lord says: 'As a mother comforts her child, so I will comfort you' (66.13) and Jesus also says, 'How often have I desired to gather your children together as a hen gathers her brood under her wings, and you were not willing!' (Matthew 23.37). In St Anselm, this image is extended:

> And you, Jesus, are you not also a mother?
> Are you not the mother, who, like a hen,
> gathers her chickens under her wings?
> Truly, Lord, you are a mother;
> for both they who are in labour
> and they who are brought forth
> are accepted by you.[18]

3.30 Mother Julian of Norwich also saw the idea of the motherhood of God standing in relation to the fatherhood of love and the lordship of the Holy Spirit. She finds in meditating on the nature of the Trinity that everything which can be said to be appropriate to the description of motherhood is found in God and that therefore it cannot be inappropriate to talk about God in this way.[19]

3.31 Some people feel that their spirituality cannot grow, or is restricted, unless they have access to this kind of language:

> I find exclusive language, talk of Christ dying 'for all men' or praying that God will bestow peace 'on all men' highly offensive. For my wife, the insistence of the Church of England, on using exclusive language while claiming that it is really inclusive, is so offensive that she finds it virtually impossible to worship using conventional prayer books or hymns.[20]

Others find inclusive language and 'politically correct' hymns and prayers undermine their understanding of Christianity and feel their ability to worship and grow similarly compromised. The Church therefore is challenged in its mission to get *beyond* this issue to the theological meaning of what is felt to be lacking or lost. Palmer's own solution is to isolate stories we must tell and stories we must drop, in order not to permit the Church to become the cause of its own alienation from people growing up and living in today's world. He also suggests that the Church is challenged to look into its roots to diagnose where the patriarchal, authoritarian expression of Christianity began, and to look at models of Christian worship and Christian theology that existed alongside this. The problem with this is that the recovery of other strands of Christian tradition may satisfy a felt need in relation to contemporary spirituality, but at the same time eclipse the processes within the mainstream tradition of Church which allow self-examination and self-criticism to promote confidence.

3.32 Some theologians, such as Matthew Fox, have attempted to address the issues of contemporary spirituality by working out a creation spirituality which is derived from early Christianity. It is 'the tradition of original blessing rather than original sin .... It is the tradition of the great mystics of the West: Hildegard, Francis, Aquinas, Eckhart, Julian of Norwich.'[21]

> Creation is original blessing, and all the subsequent blessings – those we give our loved ones and those we struggle to bring about by healing, celebration, and justice-making – are prefigured in the original blessing that creation is, a blessing so thoroughly unconditional, so fully graced, that we can go through life hardly noticing it at all.[22]

3.33 Proponents of creation spirituality argue that Christians have spent so much time working out what it means to live in a sinful, fallen world, and on Christ's redeeming work on behalf of fallen humanity, that we have forgotten the beauty, harmony and blessedness of God's intention for our life as indicated in the Creation stories. Creation spirituality therefore seeks to recover this as a present, not a past state. Such a spirituality purports to be a more holistic expression of the relationship between humankind, the environment and God.

3.34 Here, perhaps, we should not underestimate the long experience of the rural church, in which the seasonal cycle, the weather, the harvest, the influences of sun and moon all have fed into Christian practice. We may note that many of the people now encountering numinous experiences of nature and seeking to be more closely identified with the rhythms of the planet, have not themselves ever been involved in sowing or cultivating food plants or rearing and slaughtering animals. The experiences of those who have and do, within the Church and particularly in those areas of the world where food and human survival are intricately linked, may have much to inform the Church about the formation of its own creation theology. Fox suggests:

> It is ... the basic spiritual heritage of native peoples everywhere. All these peoples had cosmology as the basis of their worship, prayer, economics, politics, and morality. All of them honoured the artist in all persons. All expected the divine to burst out of anyplace [sic] at anytime [sic]. To see the world this way is to be creation centred.[23]

3.35 In Great Britain this spiritual heritage can be seen in Celtic Christianity. The Church is challenged to listen afresh to writings, prayers and hymns which celebrate God in Welsh waterfalls, Scottish moors and Irish mountains. For example, this prayer is based on the traditional words of the *Benedicite Omnia Opera* (Song of Creation):

> Hail glorious Lord! May church and chancel praise you. May church and chancel praise you.
>
> May valley floor and mountain side praise you.
>
> May the three well-springs, two above the wind and one above the earth praise you.
>
> May night and day praise you.
>
> May silk and fruit tree praise you.
>
> Abraham, founder of the faith, praised you.
>
> May eternal life praise you.
>
> May bees and birds praise you.
>
> May after-grass and fresh shoots praise you.
>
> Aaron and Moses praised you.
>
> May male and female praise you.
>
> May the seven days and the stars praise you.
>
> May the air and the upper atmosphere praise you.
>
> May books and letters praise you.
>
> May fishes in the river praise you.

> May thought and action praise you.
>
> May sand and soil praise you.
>
> May all the good that has been done praise you.
>
> I praise you, Lord of glory!
>
> Hail, glorious Lord![24]

3.36 Martin Palmer claims that the recovery of this kind of language and spiritual expression not only redresses the balance, but can have a transforming experience in our modern world of buildings and cities:

> I have cycled that route, through urban Manchester hundreds of times. That evening, as the light faded I found myself looking at it through the eyes of the Celtic Christian prayers ... suddenly I saw a world I had never seen before. It was as if through the prayers my awareness and sensitivity to all around me had been heightened to an extraordinary degree. The road I take from the office suddenly had trees and bushes I had never seen before. The pattern of the landscape was like a picture laid out for me. I found myself caught up in the space of the skies above and the movement of the rain clouds.[25]

3.37 Again, a critical view would suggest that we cannot just ignore the Church's traditional teaching about sin and fallenness. Awareness of grace in a local and personal setting may be uplifting and refreshing for the individual, but the transformation of communities must also include acknowledgement of brokenness and request for healing, as well as commitment to action.

3.38 For example, *Gaudium et Spes*, one of the documents of the Second Vatican Council, places the creation in the context of being known and experienced through the agency of the human person:

> Though made of body and soul, man is one. Through his bodily composition he gathers to himself the elements of the material world. Thus they reach their crown through him, and through him raise their voice in free praise of the Creator.
>
> For this reason man is not allowed to despise his bodily life. Rather, he is obliged to regard his body as good and hon-

ourable since God has created it and will raise it up on the last day. Nevertheless, wounded by sin, man experiences rebellious stirrings in his body. But the very dignity of man postulates that man glorify God in his body and forbid it to serve the evil inclinations of his heart.

Now, man is not wrong when he regards himself as superior to bodily concerns, and as more than a speck of nature or a nameless constituent of the city of man. For by his interior qualities he outstrips the whole sum of mere things. He finds reinforcement in this profound insight whenever he enters into his own heart. God, who probes the heart, awaits him there. There he discerns his proper destiny beneath the eyes of God. Thus, when man recognises in himself a spiritual and immortal soul, he is not being mocked by a deceptive fantasy springing from mere physical or social influences. On the contrary he is getting to the depths of the very truth of the matter.[26]

3.39 The challenge to the Church, then, is to see how far the recovery of other strands of Christian tradition can speak to those who are searching for faith, while still being engaged on an exploration of revisions which the Church must make in terms of its own traditional teachings and understanding about the nature of creation and the relation of human beings to the natural world.

3.40 This kind of understanding indicates that the spiritual longings and embryonic experiences people have are evidence that God is at work in their lives, but they may be incapable of calling on the Christian tradition to make sense of them. In the search for truth, people naturally turn to whatever seems contextually relevant, which in today's western culture is as likely to be the choice-laden offerings of therapies and practices, as the way for spiritual growth offered by the gospel. Here the Church is itself faced with a choice: does it enter into the market place and compete for the spiritual lives of human beings, or stand aloof from the quick fix alternatives which are readily available but have short shelf-lives?

3.41 *Gaudium et Spes* suggests specifically that we need to acknowledge the presence of what is evil and sinful in the world. While a life-affirming spirituality is not in itself a bad thing, it is noticeable that the need to be in control, to feel good, to have hope in the future pushes away the awkward questions the major religions seek to face: why is there suffering, poverty, injustice in the world? Contemporary spirituality may be concerned with the integrity of creation, but brokenness and imperfection are part of that creation and cannot be ignored. It is interesting in this respect that some aspects of New Age spirituality deal with evil by putting it off. Various versions of the law of karma are removed from their Hindu or Buddhist contexts, and often distorted; also belief in reincarnation, and ways of changing perception of the world, such as primal therapy (seeking out one's earliest feelings and impressions, and dealing with remembered pain by screaming or crying), colour therapy (finding out what colour combinations help you to feel relaxed and happy, or using colours as an aid to healing), and 'channelling' messages through, or meditating on, pyramids or crystals.[27] Peace and tranquillity may be installed in a person's local situation but effectively blot out responsibility to see the whole world changed. In this respect, we may say that this kind of spirituality cannot contribute to God's kingdom. It prompts us to include in our witness issues of social justice, and to make corporate effort, as the Body of Christ, to bring the world to match up to God's loving intention for all people.

Renewal

3.42 Whatever the choice, New Age practices and contemporary spirituality offer a challenge to the Church in renewal. This is not just a matter of finding a deeper and richer commitment to faith, but also a matter of the Church renewing itself by finding new ways of expressing its truths. This may mean providing prayers which address the concerns of those whose experiences are powerful and intense, but dislocated; liturgies which are expressed in language people can understand; hymns and music which can pick up and solidify the strong but often inexpressible feelings of God's presence. This does not mean throwing out what is ancient, venerable and deeply loved in our Christian tradition in exclusive favour of the trendy or culturally relevant. It does mean that there must be sensitive discernment of the need for diversity. Some manifestations of diverse ways of being Church are already noticeable, for example the music of the composer John Tavener, who seeks to convey the mystical sense of his Eastern Orthodox spirituality through walls of orchestral, especially string, sound.[28] In this way, he creates the musical equivalent of icons, as 'windows on heaven'. Arvo Pärt, by contrast, creates music of a pure, minimal variety, with much repetition, to concentrate the mind on the spiritual component of his music.[29] In other fields, the hymnody of Iona (Wild Goose Music) and Taizé allow more reflective styles of expression in worship, while Celebrating Common Prayer and the New Zealand Prayer Book are but two examples of new access for Christians into ways to pray and grow. What this also suggests is that the Church is becoming increasingly conscious of the need for a new aesthetic, in which art and nature provide the context for closer understanding of God. At the same time though, the Church is called to witness to those surrounded by ugliness and suffering, offering both solidarity with people in such conditions and the transformative power of the Holy Spirit. Fox's rejection of the 'Augustinian sin tradition' does not mean that the world is not marred, as *Gaudium et Spes* makes clear; nor should the Church offer a spirituality of goodness and beauty merely as a means of escape. In searching for ways of offering the gospel to people's emergent spiritual understanding, both the light and the dark must be held in tension.[30]

3.43   In what ways, then, can the Church respond to those who search for faith in terms of being human, of being hopeful, of needing to find grace, truth and beauty? One way, perhaps, might be for churches to commission pieces of art or sculpture, or to help people express themselves through artistic activity, such as at the Bromley-by-Bow Centre in London. The Church can also seek to mediate its missionary purpose through creative liturgies and tourist initiatives. If people walk through the door, they should find something that their own search for faith identifies with. More important, the God of our Christian witness should be recognisable as the same God who has touched those who are searching for faith but who understand the divine presence only dimly. It may be, then, that the Church also has to offer ways of praying, being and doing which promote this recognition.

3.44   In 1997, we remember the missionary journeys of St Augustine of Canterbury who arrived in Kent in 597 and also of St Columba who died in 597, and this idea of pilgrimage, in which the search for faith and the idea of journey to meet and to find come together. This may prove a helpful metaphor for ways in which Christian spirituality can commend itself to those searching for faith. This extended example from J. Philip Newell[31] may point the way forward:

> Four stations of the Iona pilgrimage provide strong images of the interwoven strands of the individual and community in relation to prayer and spirituality. The first is the practice of gathering around the highstanding cross of St Martin in front of the Abbey Church, and being reminded that the custom of the ancient Celtic Church in Scotland and Ireland was often to pray not in tightly bounded places like church sanctuaries, with their enclosing four walls and ceilings, but rather out in the great temple of creation itself. Standing together at the foot of St Martin's Cross, I was always reminded that the prayer and worship we offer is not separate from the great hymn of the universe but joins that ongoing hymn, whether it is in the rising of the morning sun, in the wind blowing over the sea or in the voice of every living creature. Spirituality should be a joining of our awareness to all that is vibrant with life, like the four living creatures of St John the Divine's vision, full of consciousness and prayerfully aware day and night in the temple of heaven and earth.

3.45 Here, J. Philip Newell directs us not to worship nature, but to join with it in the whole earth's orientation towards God the creator as envisaged in Psalm 148. Prayer and praise are not segregated from the world but present in and of the world.

> The second pilgrimage image is of visiting the ruins of the ancient hermit's cell in a not easily accessible part of the island. Situated amidst numerous little hills and across boggy terrain, many pilgrims have not been able to locate it, just as many of us have had difficulty in finding the place and the time of inner quiet and prayer in our lives. What often lies in ruins for us in the Church today is not the times of corporate worship and liturgy but the practice of contemplation and silence. There are many tales on Iona of St Columba regularly withdrawing to the hermitage to pray, and of how delighted he was to have nothing but a little pool of water to wash in, and the lark above him singing. Do we not all know the importance for our spirituality of such times of solitude, whether it is actually retreating or simply finding a quiet corner or moment of still-

ness, in order to sustain the life in community to which we are called?

3.46 This image reminds us that we are not isolated in our expression of spiritual experience. As Christians, we belong in a long line of those who have witnessed and prayed before us. Although we may need quiet and reflection, we are not shut off from the community of believers living and dead.

> The third image is of ascending the highest point on the island, Dun I, which simply means the Hill of I, or the Hill of Iona. Because of its spelling, many visitors, especially those from across the Atlantic, tended to refer to it as Dun One, which made it sound more like a lunar landing station than a hill on a Hebridean island. But, in a sense, it was that sort of perspective that we were seeking. Remember the view of earth that first became ours twenty-five years or so ago after the first moon landing. We should often gaze at the photograph of the sea-blue earth to regain our perspective. It is akin to the common biblical practice of prophets, including Jesus, going to high and remote places to be renewed in their vision. From the top of Dun I it is possible to see the White Strand of the Monks at the north of the island, where in the ninth century the abbot and fifteen monks were martyred, blood spilt on the pure white sands of Iona. Our times of withdrawal, whether it is physically to a mountain or simply to an uncluttered space, within or without, where we may see with clarity, are essential to the well-being both of our inner life and of our shared common life. And in the set apart places, it is not just to the beautiful landscape of life that we are to be looking, but to the painful and broken places as well, for it will usually be to something of the latter that we are called to return in our descent from the mountain place, or our time of interior renewal. Our spirituality, if it is to be true to life, needs to include a gazing out on the world, on both the goodness and the evil that we see in it, and to be conscious that the good and the evil are also within our own souls.

3.47 This image is important, because here we are reminded of another perspective: to see the earth in its wholeness, and we should see the darkness and brokenness as well as the light and the beauty. If we go to the mountain, we must needs come back down to the plain and resume our life. We must, as Christians, build a life of prayer in order to witness more effectively to what God has done in our social interactions and relationships. Our prayer life is therefore an extension of our being Christians and not a separate cell which is not connected to the rest of our being.

> The fourth image is that of the Reilig Oran, the Iona graveyard where Scottish Kings and Lords of the Isles are said to be buried. There the emphasis is to reflect not only on the themes of death and resurrection, of new beginnings coming out of endings in our lives and world, but on being part of those who have gone before us, who, having died, are separated from us, as George MacLeod used to say, only by a veil thin as gossamer. Part of a true spirituality is the awareness of heaven's company of light surrounding us in both the light and the darkness of earth. The ladder that connects heaven and earth, and thus the company of heaven with earth's people, is within us, and provides the flow of movement from above and below. The individualist culture of the western world has often gone hand in hand with a materialism which denies that matter is shot through with spirit, and that earth's people are enfolded by the saints and angels of heaven. Rather it sees matter and the things of earth as entirely separate from spirit and the things of heaven, if indeed it even recognizes that there is a spiritual realm. On Iona there are stories of Columba and angels of light ascending and descending on him in time of prayer. This is an image of our inner life being hid with Christ in God, enfolded in the host of light, an intimation that even in death we are not separated from one another and the saints before us.

3.48 In this image, we are reminded of the nearness of the transcendental realm and of the continuity between those who have gone before us and ourselves. This image also speaks of the recovery of a heavenly language, bringing the concepts of spirituality into the descriptions of daily life. We may also learn from theologians such as Walter Wink, who in his *Powers* trilogy brings back the language of powers and principalities to redescribe human affairs. In this view of the world, angels are not arcane beings conducting human beings to and from the astral plane as in some branches of New Age philosophy, but truly messengers, conveyers of meaning between human beings and God; they are images of right relation with God, and bearers of the promise that prayer really does act as a mode of communication between our life here and God. J. Philip Newell concludes:

> In these images of spirituality and the relationship between the individual and community, the emphasis is not on being *either* more separate or more involved, but on being *both* more separate and more involved. In our times of withdrawal and individual retreat, it is a matter of being more deeply involved in the inner heart of all humanity.

Conversion

3.49 Another way in which the Church is challenged to respond to contemporary spirituality is in and through the notion of conversion. Christian witness is required to say that those who encounter the Christ come to recognise that they are changed in a way that alters the framework and perspective of their lives. This is the origin of *metanoia*, a process of becoming that places a person's past and history in the context of a coming to know and recognise what God has done in Christ and reshapes a person's future in the context of God's promises for our ultimate destiny. We may say that this is significantly different from the spirituality of some New Age followers, with its ideal of self-realisation and emphasis on feeling good through 'quick fix' aims and practices. We have seen too that the deepening of a Christian's prayer life and Christian spirituality goes beyond casual practice of meditation or nature worship, and reaches its greatest satisfaction in the corporate worship of God, with others, and ultimately with all creation. For this reason, those quoted at the beginning of this chapter are able to articulate only a tiny piece of the larger picture, for the process of conversion to life in Christ offers the certainty of hope, the ability to face up to evil and suffering in the God who suffers with us, obviates the need to try and control our local world to our own ends and offers a lasting joy and peace beyond the quick fix remedy. The Church is therefore challenged to make these distinctions to those who search for faith, and to encourage those whose emerging spirituality is made manifest, to build on these beginnings for the 'life in all its fullness' promised in St John's Gospel (e.g. John 10.10).

Conclusion

3.50 Contemporary spirituality offers a number of important challenges to the Church. However, mission theology provides an important insight into how these challenges can be addressed.

3.51 First, the idea that the missionary God affirms every human person helps to provide a basis on which to reach out to those people identified by research such as that done by the Alister Hardy Research Centre. People who have a religious awareness, no matter how poorly articulated, may be seen to be already touched, or disturbed by God, and Christian experience can similarly affirm and ally with such experience. Further, this allows us to distinguish between affirmation of the self as good, but self-centredness as being antithetical to the gospel. The sensations of power and control which are associated with the individualistic attitudes of today have therefore to be dealt with and appropriately assimilated within our interpretation of the gospel.

3.52 Similarly, mission theology allows us to speak to a desire to affirm the whole body as God's good creation, just as Jesus Christ was himself en-human-ed, and that orthopraxis, the right way to behave in respect of our bodies, is given to us in Jesus's own example. For Jesus himself was made known to us as a human being as the creed says [*enanthropesanta*], and made known to us as a man. In this way, 'the Word was made flesh and dwelt among us full of grace and truth' (John 1.14). Mission theology gives us the tools to describe God's future according to his promises, allowing the human need to hope to be poured into this and located in the vision of his glory.

3.53 By affirming this vision, the awareness of evil and of the brokenness of the world can be addressed. What is significant here is the need to see this as a contemporary meaningful vision, not an outdated fantasy. We also need to develop a more robust form of creation theology which appropriately locates contemporary planet-related spirituality. Consequently, we need to be seen to be not just reacting to contemporary spirituality in 'too little, too late' mode, but actively leading the way in making the Church the natural place where these spiritual journeys can be continued.

Summary

KEY WORDS

- spirituality
- transcendence
- numinous
- complementary medicine
- spiritual direction
- holism
- New Age
- exclusive language
- creation spirituality
- Celtic spirituality
- renewal
- conversion

There is a commonly understood sense that 'being religious' is not restricted to attending a place of religious worship. Spiritual experience is common to all human beings, whether they acknowledge it as such or not. Research shows that descriptions of such experiences carry certain themes. First, the experience is highly personal and concentrated back on the individual, not the corporate nature of the experience. Second, the enhanced sense of self occasioned by such experiences raises expectations of being in control of one's destiny, whether that is in partnership with God or perceived as a need to reject God. Third, experiences underline the need to feel good about oneself, not just in terms of mental confidence, but in terms of the body, its health, its appearance, its sexuality. Fourth, people are greatly concerned with the future and a need to find means of generating hope. Fifth, there is an increased concern for, and interest in, the natural world, and a sense that our place within creation is an important matter which requires addressing.

Many people who experience their spirituality in this way look around to find contextually relevant ways of furthering their spiritual growth. They are faced with and attracted by the many ways of doing this offered by our choice-ridden, quick fix market culture. In particular they may opt for New Age-style practices, alternative therapies, or adopt a mixture of ideas, rituals and philosophies. Some may eventually find their way into a permanent home with one of the major world religions, which may or may not include Christianity.

The Church is therefore challenged to offer the Gospel of Jesus Christ into these spiritual experiences and spiritual journeys, but in doing so it needs to be sure about its faithfulness to Scripture and tradition and not merely compete for people's attention. For this reason, there is renewed interest in working out a theology for creation spirituality, for the ministry of healing, for forms of spiritual expression which draw on traditions such as Celtic spirituality. In these ways, the mission of God's love to the world is advanced by offering an holistic vision of spiritual growth, which people may turn to for a permanent and enduring home for their experience, not just an immediate gratification, and which allows them room to grow for all of their life.

Further reading

Cracknell, Kenneth, *Towards a New Relationship: Christians and People of Other Faith*, Epworth, 1986.

Fox, Matthew, *Creation Spirituality: Liberating Gifts for the Peoples of the Earth*, HarperCollins, 1991.

Gaudium et Spes, Documents of Vatican II, *The Church Today*.

Palmer, Martin, *Living Christianity*, Element, 1993.

Thomas, Patrick, *Candle in the Darkness: Celtic Spirituality from Wales*, Gomer Press, 1993.

Further information can also be obtained from:

The Alister Hardy Research Centre*
Westminster College
Oxford

*(Alister Hardy Trust and Religious Experience Research Centre)

The world is my oyster

Things to do

- **AIM:** to look at some elements of contemporary spirituality concerning God and the natural world and to see how the Church can respond positively as well as critically to them.
- **PURPOSE:** to find ways of reaching out to people through their expressions of spirituality.

BIBLE VERSE

> Let us hold fast to the confession of our hope without wavering, for he who has promised is faithful. (Hebrews 10.23)

Things to do include:

a. Thinking about pleasurable things
b. Reading a poem
c. Looking at a picture
d. Looking at images or advertisements
e. Discussion starters
f. Singing hymns

1. FAVOURITE THINGS

Ask people in pairs to write down their favourite foods, favourite scents, favourite piece of music, favourite clothing material, favourite colour.

Write them up on a chart. Do any of these have anything to do with the Church? Discuss ways in which our favourite things might lead us to encounter and form relationships with those outside the Church.

2. A POEM

Ask someone to read the poem aloud, or let the group read it to themselves.

God's Grandeur

The world is charged with the grandeur of God.
It will flame out like shining from shook foil;
It gathers to a greatness, like the ooze of oil
Crushed. Why do men then now not reck his rod?
Generations have trod, have trod, have trod;
And all is seared with trade; bleared, smeared with toil;
And wears man's smudge and shares man's smell: the soil
Is bare now, nor can foot feel being shod.

And for all this, nature is never spent;
There lives the dearest freshness deep down things;
And though the last lights off the black West went
Oh, Morning, at the brown brink eastward, springs –
Because the Holy Ghost over the bent
World broods with warm breast and with ah! bright wings.

(Poems and Prose of Gerard Manley Hopkins,
(ed.) W. H. Gardener, Penguin, 1953, p.27)

Ask people to get into pairs and to talk about the words in the poem.

Questions for group discussion:
- Do you understand the poem?
- What do you think the poem tells us about nature? About God?
- Have you had an experience of God's grandeur? What happened?
- What Bible passages link with these poems?

3. PICTURES

Ask the whole group: what does this image say to you (see Figure 6)?

The world is my oyster

Figure 6 Verbum © 1996 M.C. Escher. Cordon Art, Baarn, Holland. All rights reserved.

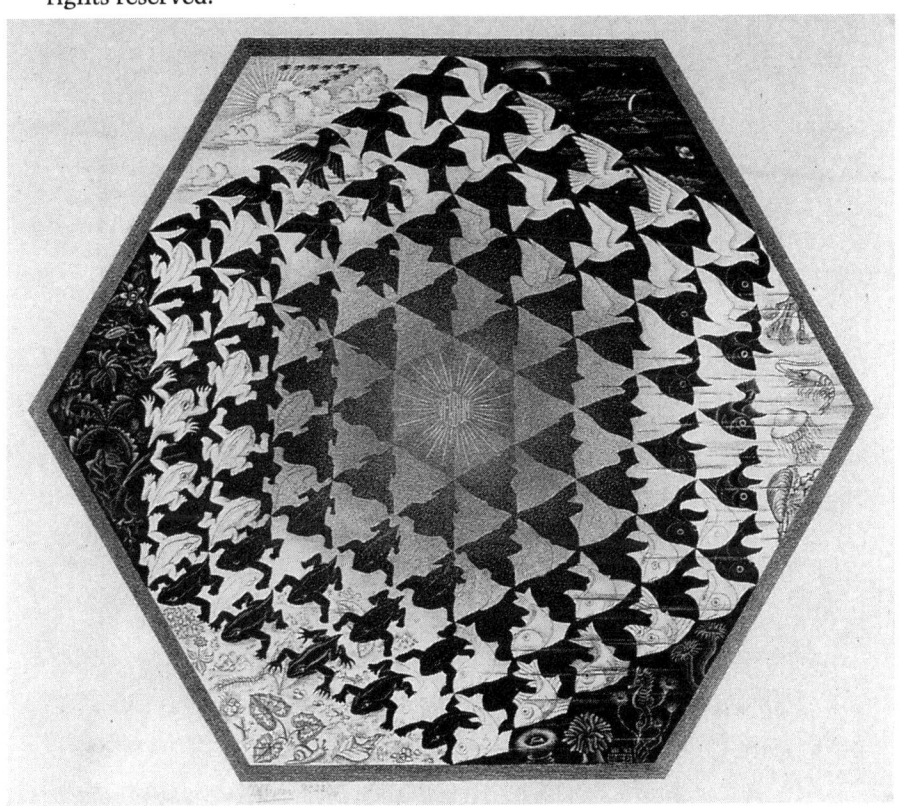

In pairs, discuss how we can get across our understanding of God's relation to the natural world to people who think nature and God are the same thing. (This can also be discussed in relation to the poem.)

You could also cut out magazine or holiday brochure pictures of beautiful places and ask how these make people feel. Then try images of destruction and decay. Which ones make people think most readily of God?

Think about how we can help people find God in *any* situation.

4. ADVERTISEMENTS

Look at advertisements in magazines or the local paper for various therapies or New Age practices. Also look at instructions on e.g. aromatherapy oils, etc.

Ask people in small groups to talk about which they may have tried or would like to try. Which ones would people definitely not try? Why not?

5. DISCUSSION STARTERS

Choose a question or questions that are relevant to your group. Ask people to discuss in pairs and then contribute two ideas to a whole group discussion.

a. Do you have to go to church to be religious?

b. How do personal experiences of transcendence or the nearness of God fit with being a church community?

c. Do you think people searching for faith have already been touched by God? If so, how should we talk to them about the gospel?

d. Is the sense of self-worth a religious experience? Is the Church responsible for damaging people's sense of self-worth?

e. Is it important to feel good about yourself, your appearance, your body? Does the Church contribute to this?

f. Are therapies and New Age practices bad for your spiritual health? Or are there practices and therapies from which Christians may benefit?

g. Should the Church develop its healing ministry within services?

h. Is the Church failing to preach a message of hope?

i. Does the Church need creation spirituality? Can different spiritualities enrich the Church?

j. What should our attitude be towards those who find a spiritual home in other faiths?

6. MUSIC

Sing a Taizé chant such as *Ubi Caritas* or a quiet hymn you use in your church or group. Ask people what effect the music and the words have.

Does it help you to feel close to each other, to God, or to pray?

Ask people how they think we can reach out to people searching for faith through our music. Or consider this hymn: 'This web of words and images' (tune: Ellacombe or Kingsfold).

The world is my oyster

This web of words and images,
This net of sight and sound,
This linking of humanity,
By space and time un-bound,
Leaves God bemused, for what excites
Each possibility,
Was grounded in creation's form
At time's nativity.

We download data, file or fax,
Through cyberspace we probe;
We surf the net, we browse the web,
We navigate the globe;
And God observes, involved within
The body that he wove:
Joined by a net that's limitless
Whose access code is love.

We glance, we merely glimpse a part
That all creation holds;
We tinker with infinity,
Eternity unfolds;
Before the internet, the web,
The highway was in place,
The Word, God's cosmic interface,
Gave form to time and space.

(Andrew E. Pratt)

Discuss what this modern hymn says to people.

Notes

1. Edward Robinson and Michael Jackson, *Religion and Values at Sixteen Plus*, Alister Hardy Research Centre, Christian Education Movement, 1987, p.73.
2. These three examples come from ibid., p.17.
3. Ibid., p.19.
4. Ibid., p.20.
5. In Martin Forward's paper on The New Age Movement, for the Faith and Order Committee of the Methodist Conference, he points to 'the emphasis on the individual and the individual's right or ability to select from all that is on offer the mix that is appropriate for them' (p.4).
6. Mary Loudon, *Revelations: The Clergy Questioned*, Penguin edition, 1995, p.20.
7. See, for example, Kenneth Cracknell, *Towards a New Relationship*, Epworth, 1986, pp.98ff.
8. *Religion and Values*, op. cit., p.20.
9. Ibid., p.22.
10. W. B. Yeats, *Collected Poems*, Macmillan edition, 1979, p.284. In this poem Yeats rejects Christianity for the richness of the pre-Christian experience, as represented by 'Homer and his unchristened heart'.
11. For example, see the Revd Mike Starkey, *Fashion and Style*, Monarch, 1995. Are Christianity and looking good incompatible?
12. *Brave New World*, 1932, Penguin edition, 1995.
13. Julie Burchill, 'The Religion for the Me Generation', *Sunday Times*, 15 October 1995.
14. The 'Gaia' hypothesis in which the whole planet is seen as a self-regulating organism, was advanced by Professor James Lovelock.
15. Andrew Marvell, 'On Drop of Dew', in James Reeves and Martin Seymour-Smith (eds), *The Poems of Andrew Marvell*, Heinemann, 1969, pp.18–19.
16. R. S. Thomas, 'The Other', in *Collected Poems, 1945–1990*, Phoenix edition, 1995, p.457.
17. The St Hilda Community, *Women Included: A Book of Services and Prayers*, SPCK, 1991, p.45.
18. 'Prayer to St Paul' in *The Prayers and Meditations of St Anselm*, Penguin edition, 1973, p.153.
19. Julian of Norwich, *Revelations of Divine Love*, Penguin edition, 1966, especially chapters 57–63.
20. Martin Palmer, *Living Christianity*, Element, 1993, p.139.
21. Interview in *Third Way*, June 1995, p.17.
22. Matthew Fox, *Creation Spirituality: Liberating Gifts for the Peoples of the Earth*, HarperCollins, 1991, p.11.
23. Ibid., p.14.

24. See Patrick Thomas, *Candle in the Darkness: Celtic Spirituality from Wales*, Gomer Press, 1993, p.139. (Translation by Patrick Thomas from the Welsh.)
25. Palmer, op. cit., p.80.
26. The Documents of Vatican II, *The Church Today*, 14.
27. For further information about these various practices and therapies, see Eileen Campbell and J. H. Brennan, *Dictionary of Body, Mind and Spirit: Ideas, People and Places*, Aquarian Press (HarperCollins), revised edition, 1994.
28. For example, *The Protecting Veil* (1987), or *We Shall See Him as He Is* (1990) (text by Mother Thekla, Abbess of the Orthodox Monastery in Normanby, Tavener's friend and spiritual adviser).
29. For example, *Passio* (1982).
30. So in Sir Michael Tippett's oratorio *A Child of our Time* (1944), the final section begins with the words 'I would know my shadow and my light, so shall I at last be whole' until the work ends in the affirmation of the spiritual *Deep River*.
31. J. Philip Newell, 'Spirituality, Community and an Individualist Culture', in *Teaching Spirituality, The Way*, Supplement 1995/84, Autumn 1995, pp.123–5.

4

Why world? Why oysters?

My name's Sally. I'm into science. What I like about it is the way everything's being discovered and worked out. It's so wonderful what scientists are doing to tell us the answers to the big questions and when I think about it, the universe seems so big, so beautiful, so empty. Scientists are finding everything out, even down to the way a butterfly affects all the weather systems of the world. You don't need God in all that. It's like evolution: everything happens by chance and we're here only because our genes need bodies to survive in. Sorry God, you're out of date on that. I don't think you need the transcendent stuff cluttering everything up; the circle of life is complete.

I don't want to start trying to match up people's Christian faith with what the scientists say. I'll put my faith in the great technological advances we've got now; that's got to be better than prayer!

The Church shouldn't interfere. Religion is just an invention to stop us being frightened of death. I'm happy with the knowledge we've got nowadays. God's been pushed in a corner and he'll soon disappear altogether, right? The Church is always looking backwards, but we've got to push on into the undiscovered country.

Introduction

Many people who think that religious belief is no longer relevant to twentieth-century living do so because they see scientific advance in a highly technological society as able to provide answers to all modern problems and questions. Other people feel faced with a choice between religious and scientific worldviews, or that science belongs in the public world, especially where they encounter 'popular science' and that religion belongs only to the realm of private opinion, to be kept under wraps.

The Christian Church, then, has to face up to a challenge to show its witness to be complementary to the scientific worldview. The Church has an opportunity to point to a view we have forgotten, in which relationship with God guides and frames our attempts to make discoveries through our scientific abilities. As cosmologists attempt to describe the universe more and more completely, we must not allow God to become merely the God-of-the-gaps. In the quantum world, we believe God to be there as the sustaining presence, even where there are limits placed on our observations. Similarly, the life scientists challenge the Church to make sense of evolution, and to promote our vision of what God is calling us to be.

The Church is also challenged to bring its witness into the complex situations created by today's technology. Where human beings have the power to bring about life in a test tube and to keep alive those who cannot sustain their own lives independently, the Church can offer something of its own view of life and death where people are asked to face increasingly difficult decisions.

This chapter examines what the Church can say in all these circumstances, which highlights our missionary task to be the people of God's future.

Science and the search for faith

Science without religion is lame, religion without science is blind.[1]

The whole history of science has been the gradual realization that events do not happen in an arbitrary manner, but that they reflect a certain underlying order, which may or may not be divinely inspired.[2]

Why?

4.1   It is in the nature of most human beings to ask fundamental questions about themselves and about the world. Why are we here? How did the world begin? When will the world end? Why am I as I am?

4.2   When we consider these questions, we can see that there are different categories of question: questions relating to the self, questions relating to the world and questions relating to the universe. There are also different kinds of expected answer: answers of fact, which effectively decline the question, answers of accommodation, which do not 'solve' the question but point towards a helpful conclusion, and complementary answers which provide the questioner with different levels of satisfaction and which provide different frames of reference and perception. It is this last category which will become important in our discussions in this chapter.

4.3 The majority of known religions include a narrative or story which is designed to explain how the world and human beings came into being; what our relations are with the transcendental realm and what is likely to happen to us when we die. We have already made reference to these narratives in the Christian tradition in Chapter 2. These narratives are not straight answers, but stories which can be given orally, remembered and passed on. Who and what human beings are passes into the narrated history of a people. Anthropologists have given us many descriptions of how such stories carry an important means of sense-making for people, generating art, ritual and meaning for daily life. What is pre-eminent in such stories is the existence of the transcendent and the centrality and importance of human beings in relationship with the transcendent realm. When modern science seems to challenge both these important elements, we have to consider carefully the effect on our ability to make sense of what we know, experience or believe.

4.4 Consequently, when Christians tell the Good News of what God has done for us through salvation history and quintessentially in Jesus Christ, we speak of things which emanate from the history of the Jewish people and from a world-changing event nearly 2,000 years ago. Christian writers, theologians and philosophers have been trying to refine our understanding of what took place then, ever since, and to relate this to contemporary situations. In doing so, Scripture and tradition are basic tools for our understanding.

4.5 Christians, then, have had answers to fundamental questions about human life, which relate directly to our understanding of the work of God in history. The framework of understanding which Christian faith provides is given to us as a narrative: the history of God's saving work. The churches have developed a story of creation, a story of the way God relates to human beings, a story of the end-time and of God's intentions for human beings.

Across the whole breadth of the Christian Church theological approaches to these matters vary, but broadly speaking, the Christian confession of belief is set down in the historic creeds agreed and summarised at the four great Councils of the Church (AD 325–451) (see Chapter 5) and is still said by Christians in their churches today.

4.6   When we say the creed, we assent to a particular understanding of why things are as they are. We assent: to God's creatorship of all that is known to us and ever will be known to us; to God's missionary action in reaching out and acting in history; to his supreme act of self-revelation in Christ; to God's plan for all that has been created: the kingdom without end. Our very ability to ask questions can be seen as an act of God-seeking or God-pointing, whether we discover God through our questions or not.

4.7   The processes of secularisation and individualisation, however, mean that for many people today access to this kind of perceptual frame is missing. For example, in the face of knowledge about the human genome, and even fairly elementary knowledge of genetics, the virgin birth of a male child may appear simply too unbelievable. Many people have had no contact with the kind of epistemological base offered by the Church or by any other belief system, and therefore have no way of dealing with this kind of truth claim. Many people simply do not get to hear what the Church has to say about these matters, or if they do, they do not believe it. Why is this? What can the Church do about it? Is it that the Scriptures, the creeds, the witness of Christians are simply not enough to those who search and ask questions? Is it that people have access to other systems for sense-making which crowd out the Christian perspective, that are ultimately chosen over the Christian, or other religious ones? Is it further that the Christian, or, indeed, any other religious perspective is no longer brought into people's lives early enough, so that faith development is marred or deflected by the satisfaction of answers obtained from other disciplines? Are the *first* answers the ones which lay down the sense-making apparatus for people's lives? If so, the place of religion in education becomes paramount.

4.8   In order to respond to these questions, which are crucial for the mission of the Church, we need to look at the places where people find answers that satisfy their needs. In this chapter, we will look at the perspectives offered by science.

4.9   In the first place we must distinguish between science and 'scientism'. That is to say, many people are satisfied by explanations called 'scientific' but which bear little relation to the actual science involved, which may be very complex and provide a variety of information rather than one 'answer'. One example of a scientistic point of view is the popular misconception that science and Christian faith have been at loggerheads for centuries. However, this idea of a continuous conflict stems from a nineteenth-century rewriting of history. There is also a view that 2,000 years of Christian thought have been sidelined by advances in the sciences. Christianity, and religion in general, are sometimes seen as a marginal refuge for those who cannot quite hold on to the scientific revolutions of the twentieth century.

4.10   It is a fact of our present western culture that, while many people do not have exposure to the basic stories about Jesus, the majority do have good access to scientific ideas. Television programmes like *Tomorrow's World* and *Horizon*, radio programmes such as *Science Now*, and science articles in newspapers give the general public access to complex scientific ideas, and provide entry points for learning about matters of particular interest or concern. Such matters might include the understanding of the structure and transmission of the Human Immunodeficiency Virus (HIV); the development of the information technology and computer culture; the mechanisation of society, with continuing advances in robotics and automation in industry; the probable origin of the universe in the Big Bang. The strong interest in gaining general access to otherwise specialist areas of scientific study and analysis is demonstrated by the phenomenal success of Professor Stephen Hawking's book *A Brief History of Time*, and of a host of other 'popular science' books.

Three consequences

4.11   First, we can see the consequences of the scientific discussions and advances of the nineteenth and twentieth centuries in terms of a general addition to our understanding and capability. We now understand the part that evolution has had to play in shaping our minds and bodies and this has led us to examine our own genetic make-up; we understand the huge expanse of the universe in terms of general relativity and the sub-atomic world in terms of quantum theory. We use lasers in surgery and compact disc players; we use computers to write, calculate and communicate; we have the ability to travel in space and explore our solar system by remote control; we have advanced medical techniques and machinery to produce and to preserve life, even to the point of engineering the DNA evolution has given us. We can even try to make sense of the world around us through the mathematics of chaos and complexity theories, and so to relate everything around us to ourselves.

4.12 Second, through dedication to scientific advance, it seems that human beings have the ability to penetrate the secrets of almost anything within reach. This fuels the view that anything strange, mysterious or unknown can be made accessible to humans as long as there are resources for adequate technology to be put in place. There is, as it were, 'nothing sacred'.

4.13 Third, people can be seen to place faith and hope in a future in which science has solved the ills of the world and overcome the limitations of human beings. One day, perhaps, there will be a 'cure' for cancer; pollution-free synthetics will return the earth to its original cleanness; people will travel to the stars and create new paradises. Against this is set the other side of human behaviour: advances in science and technology permit the creation of the Semtex explosive, and provide more sophisticated methods of waging war and committing crime. Science may 'work', but it can also have frightening consequences. With scientific advance come important questions about accountability.

4.14 The majority of people have some idea of these advances, if not through education or the media, then through experience of technology in daily life. The matter of science teaching in schools is of particular importance, since most schoolchildren have exposure to classroom science through its significance within the National Curriculum. We therefore have to ask whether or not the prominence of science teaching leads to the description of a particular worldview (which may not be particularly scientific) becoming the dominant one for young minds. There are two important points arising from this which have consequences for the mission of the Church. The first is that people receive more knowledge about the scientific perspective than they do about the religious perspective and their ability to compare those perspectives and gauge their satisfaction is impaired. This naturally raises questions about the place of religious education and about catechesis and whether teaching the Christian faith to those whose exposure to its story has been minimal is made more difficult by what they may have learned through other disciplines, as Craig Raine suggests:

> I never liked God, but struggled with him
>
> like algebra and trigonometry.[3]

4.15 Second, popular modes of encounter with scientific ideas do not for the most part address the role of religion or religious belief along with the scientific contribution. Consequently, and however mistakenly, there often emerges a perception that science and religion are somehow incompatible, or actually competing with each other. There are various reasons for this. For example:

1. Science may appear to *displace* or *undermine* religious understanding. For example, steady state models of the universe in which energy comes into existence out of nothing and Stephen Hawking's 'no-boundary' proposition suggest that in these models of the creation of the universe there would have been nothing for a Creator God to do.[4]

2. Science may appear to *disprove* matters of faith. For example, when the religious authorities presented the Turin Shroud for testing, the result of this test (if it was accurate) appeared to 'prove' it to be a medieval fake and therefore 'disproved' the hope that it is Christ's burial sheet. For some people, this also meant that science had disproved the resurrection of Jesus. In fact, it is still not clear how the Turin Shroud came into existence; people are not generally aware of the existence of other shrouds and also do not always understand that carbon dating cannot make any difference to the truth of the resurrection.

3. Science may appear to *explain away* miracles and collapse experiences of transcendence. For example, in his book on migraine, Dr Oliver Sacks shows that the 'visions' experienced by Hildegard of Bingen and interpreted by her as religious experiences, were most likely caused by typical migrainous scotoma – disturbances of vision, typified by flashing lights and bright patterns before the eyes.[5] The

historical evidence for miracles may appear so flimsy that people today cannot find any meaning in them, either as events or as contexts.

4. Science *enters into* areas typically thought to be in God's hands. For example, doctors can bring about human life *in vitro*, and preserve the vital functions of the brain dead through life support machines.

Choices: either/or

4.16 It is not surprising, then, that people who are searching for faith and looking to see what the witness of the Church can do for their search, sometimes find themselves in positions where they may think they have to choose between a 'scientific' explanation of the world and our place in it and a 'religious' explanation of the creation and our role in it. There is further the added suggestion, sometimes, that the holders of the religious view do so 'against the evidence'. It is perfectly true that there are scientists such as Peter Atkins who may see the world as beautiful and ordered, but entirely mechanistic and clockwork and whose reductionist view of the world leaves no room for God or for true humanity or for any kind of belief.[6] On the other hand, there are also people who choose the religious view so exclusively as to reject what science can tell us altogether. Creationists, for example, believe in the literal truth of the creation stories in Genesis, and do not accept ideas about the age of the universe, or that animals, plants and human beings evolved. Yet is the either/or distinction necessary? In recent years there have been a number of books by scientists who are also Christian believers, demonstrating from their own intellectual position that there is no contradiction in terms.[7] The mathematician Abdus Salam, who refers to himself as a Muslim, finds no conflict at all, seeing a directive in the Qur'an to study nature and to find the signs of God in nature.[8]

4.17 In addition, Bishop Hugh Montefiore suggests:

> There are aspects of the natural sciences which are not dissimilar to those of religion. For example, both inherit a tradition, and in both trust is needed in that tradition. There are other aspects which are very different. Faith in God is different from a mere hypothesis about God. While religions may hope to refine or develop their systems of belief, faith in God is not regarded as provisional in the sense that a better hypothesis is

forthcoming. For the most part the natural sciences are concerned with a different question from that of religion.[9]

Complementarity

4.18 If, through their traditions, science and Christian faith can be said to address similar big issues which are of concern to ordinary people, then we can begin with the premise that science and religious belief, including Christianity, are not as incompatible or mutually exclusive as they may sometimes appear to be. They may be becoming more compatible as our understanding increases. Science and Christianity may each contribute to the process of giving satisfying responses to complex questions about ourselves and the world we live in. Nor is this merely a defensive argument, saying that no matter how much scientists discover and explain, Christianity will never be displaced, rather, it is a confidence that the longer scientists spend on their investigations, the more likely they are to need to start thinking about God. This is true of the thought of Paul Davies, for instance (winner of the 1995 Templeton prize), whose claim is that 'science offers a surer path than religion in the search of God'.[10] What does this mean, though? For Christians this suggestion may not go far enough, for knowledge of God or the search for faith does not mean response to God or participation in worship. The mission question for the Church here, then, is to give people (scientists included) a deeper understanding of God and the divine work in creation as part of a larger truth which is none the less often overlooked. Some scientists who mention God in their popular books, talk in an unconstructed deistic way. That is, they categorise God as a function, such as creator, without reference to God's relationship with human beings or, indeed, God's missionary purpose of sending love into the world. We can provide more, not just through academic theology, but through the experiences of Christians in the everyday world. This means that those who search for faith do not have to be torn between choices; Christianity and science can be seen as complementary in offering different considerations of what we know. Further complementarity itself points to a more complete understanding of ourselves in creation. We examine this under two headings below.

How far complementarity? (i) The whole person in medical science

4.19 Addressing the whole person is not a new concept, as we have seen in Chapter 3. We might do well to remember that, in the western world at least, science has emerged from roots in religious understanding. The Wellcome Museum of Medicine in the Science Museum in London demonstrates the close relationship between medical research through the centuries and the search for a healing that was not just physical, but spiritual. Often remedies and prayers were integrated in the treatment. Without the kind of understanding of anatomy and physiology which modern medicine has today, whole person medicine was developed and practised, on which a stronger focus is gradually being recovered today.

4.20 For example, ancient treatment for a snake bite would first include drawing out the poison and applying a poultice or other medication. Yet there would also be a prayer or other form of words to focus the patient's mind on getting rid of the poison in the body. The treatment might also include confrontation with a real snake (maybe *the* snake) or an image of it to confirm healing from the event and to restore the world in which snakes and humans do not injure each other.[11] An example of this in the Bible is the brazen serpent of Numbers 21.9 where the Lord tells Moses how to treat snake bite: 'Moses made a serpent of bronze, and put it upon a pole; and whenever a serpent bit someone, that person would look at the serpent of bronze and live.' Modern treatment for phobias may also include confrontation with the source of the fear (desensitisation). Another example of how holistic medicine is being recovered today would be the practice of giving patients control over their own pain relief, giving them freedom from anxiety about pain and control over their illness.

4.21 The Christian tradition developed the Ignatian idea of the eucharist as *pharmakon*, the remedy given to us by Christ the Healer. Emphasis was placed, not just on dealing with injury or with disease, but on recovery of right relationship with God. The family therapist Jeremy Woodcock, writing of his experience of assisting those who have suffered human rights violations, agrees with Anne Nasimiyu-Wasike that the image of Christ the Healer is precisely what is required by many African women. For them, T. S. Eliot's paradox 'The wounded surgeon plies the steel', the healer who suffers our wounds himself in solidarity with us, is a source of hope: 'Beneath the bleeding hands we feel/The sharp compassion of the healer's art/Resolving the enigma of the fever chart.'[12] Because God has suffered in Christ, healing is related to compassion and mercy for the sufferer, beyond the physical damage sustained by the body. Further, the idea of *pharmakon* is not restricted to Christianity:

> On the anniversary of executions in their family, I suggest to a [Muslim] couple that they bring the halvah into the Medical Foundation to share in solidarity with the suffering of others. Halvah is the confection of honey and sesame seeds which it is traditional to bake and offer to others with a blessing.[13]

4.22 In considering a whole person approach to medicine, there also has to be preserved the proper balance between the activity of God and medical skill:

> When the surgery was completed and Margaret returned from hospital to our home remarkably quickly and feeling surprisingly well, friends assured us that it was all down to their prayers. We had been supported, we knew, by a considerable volume of prayer and we were extremely grateful for it. Nevertheless their response to Margaret's recovery was a little irritating. It seemed to demean the efforts of the surgeon and his support staff. He was superbly sensitive and understanding in all our meetings with him, ready to explain each stage carefully and to answer all our questions in a straightforward manner. As far as we could tell, the surgery had been carried out with great skill. All the good things we had heard about him in advance were confirmed in our experience. We could not now deny that and give all the credit to God and our praying supporters. The surgeon's professionalism and care must be given proper notice in any understanding of providence at work in the situation. [But] ... It may be that the totality of our experience during Margaret's illness would have been different without prayer.[14]

4.23 Here, Mervyn Willshaw considers how it is possible to hold together scientific skill and Christian faith in an inclusive way. His reference to the totality of the experience of his wife's illness and treatment reminds us that illness, suffering and pain are not things which are passed over into the scientist's hands when God has failed, nor things to be passed back to hope of a miracle when doctors and technology fail. Rather, the placing of an artificial distinction between the activity of God and the activity of the doctors needs to be eroded. We may look at the advances made by the hospice movement today as recovering the balance between medical treatment of the body and mental and spiritual requirements. Offering the opportunity to die well and with dignity, using pain-relieving drugs to enhance quality of life rather than its length is seen as responding to the needs of the whole person rather than just 'the patient'.

How far complementarity? (ii) Cosmological discovery and the Church

> Man has measured the heavens with a telescope
> Driven the gods from their thrones
>
> (Michael Tippett, *A Child of our Time*, oratorio)

4.24 Just as medicine demonstrates an historical closeness between science and faith, so the study of the heavens and the discovery of the position and status of the earth in relation to the solar system, the galaxy and, indeed, the universe was set in the context of a theological and metaphysical understanding which exercised a powerful hold on the minds and imaginations of people, including the scientists. This led to a highly complex historical situation, but the religious view defining human beings and God, earth and heaven, was often perceived to be so dominant that the scientific view about actual observation was declared to be incompatible, leading to persecution and charges of heresy.[15] Yet often the religious view had encouraged scientific enterprise, and many scientists worked with explicitly religious presuppositions.

How far complementarity now?

4.25 Today, we can see that the history of western physical science has required a series of large leaps of conscious understanding. Not only have we had to accept the loss of the idea that the existence of humankind is central and pre-eminent (although some of this is now being reconsidered), but we have to accommodate the complex mathematics of describing time and space, and the need to imagine all events as relative to one another. Einstein's theory of general relativity which suggested that there is no one privileged platform for observation of physical events has consequences for our philosophical enquiries. There is perhaps also the sense that science has advanced and changed so radically while Christian faith, as, for example, set down in the creeds, has remained in the same place, old-fashioned, outdated and irrelevant. We need to admit that new models of the universe and scientific discoveries challenge our ideas of God and encourage us to think about God in a new way.

4.26 The challenge here to the Church is to show that while Christians still hold to the central doctrines of Christian faith, the amount we know and understand about God's mission of love to the world may also change with time and human experience. We really do have new things to say to today's world, even if the foundations for our faith are unchanging, for these are born out of our exciting and creative interactions with new knowledge, especially that arising from scientific enterprise.

4.27 This means that Christianity is not a fossilised religion, but is continuously remaking itself in creative and fresh ways. We are challenged to fill our language with new pictures, metaphors and stories which allow us to make our description of the way the world is and about our place in it more referential of God. We are challenged to represent what we believe God has done and will do, as set out in the creed, and draw on all current sources of knowledge to enrich that belief for others. In particular, Christians have three things to offer:

4.28 We have a view of our future which generates hope: *he will come again in glory ... and his kingdom will have no end*. In the fulfilment of God's promises, Jesus Christ will be with us again in a world which is created and experienced in accordance with God's will.

4.29 We have a way of understanding that is personal and relevant: *for us ... and for our salvation he came down from heaven ... and became truly human* (English Language Liturgical Consultation). Jesus, God incarnate, became a human being and shared our life.

4.30 We have a way of describing reality in terms of value, purpose and meaningfulness: *for our sake he was crucified ... and rose again*. Jesus died, as we do, but he rose from the dead to show us that we have an eternal destiny and a meaning and value in God's eyes which extends beyond our death.

4.31 Why should these perspectives be of any use, when science can give us deeply satisfying and beautiful explanations? In order to illustrate this at a general level we may look at the description of a kiss, which allows us to use language in a metaphorical way that will be helpful in the following parts of this chapter. A 'scientific' description might suggest that a kiss signifies the approach of two pairs of lips with the exchange of carbon dioxide and microbes, and contraction of the orbicular muscles. But such a description would be meaningless to two people whose purpose in, and experience of, kissing would be in terms of value, enrichment, love. Both descriptions might be true, but would give a different satisfaction in terms of the answer to the question: 'What is a kiss?' It is also clear that it is the latter description which provides the most information about what a kiss means for a person, for relationships and for a person's future.[16]

4.32 In the following paragraphs, we will consider in very brief outline some of the topics which people often regard as challenging to the Christian faith and see what issues are raised by these advances to the mission of the Church and how the Church may respond.

The natural sciences

ORIGINS

- I believe in God, the Father almighty, maker of heaven and earth, of all things seen and unseen.

- The idea that space and time may form a closed surface without boundary also has profound implications for the role of God in the affairs of the universe ... So long as the universe had a beginning, we could suppose it had a creator. But if the universe is really completely self-contained, having no boundary or edge, it would have neither beginning nor end: it would simply be. What place, then, for a creator?[17]

- I, even my hands, have stretched out the heavens. (Isaiah 45.12)

4.33 When we ask the question, 'How did it all begin?', cosmologists currently tell us that the universe 'began' in what is known as the Big Bang: a vast explosion out of which came everything we now observe in the universe, and possibly more that we cannot observe at all. There is much evidence for the idea that there really was a Big Bang, but it is very difficult to discover what happened right at the very first moment (if there was a first moment). So what was before the Big Bang? We are told the question has no meaning, since time and space emerged together at the Big Bang. What we know is that the universe is expanding and is now very big indeed; our local patch of the universe is far away from the origin in time.

4.34 People who are searching for faith, whose perception of God is weak or unformed, are sometimes perplexed by Christians' claim to believe in a Creator God, when science seems to have shown that such an idea is unnecessary. What people sometimes fail to grasp is that a belief in the 'maker of heaven and earth' does not commit us to the view that the universe has a beginning. However, what tends to happen when people grapple with these ideas, is the formation of a 'God-in-the-gaps' theology. That is, whatever is as yet unknown by the scientists can be left to the 'hand of God'. Gradually, as more and more is known, God's role shrinks away until finally the 'Creator' evaporates altogether. There is simply nothing, as Stephen Hawking has mooted, for God to do.

4.35 This way of thinking, however, can also lead to a picture of God in which God lights the blue touchpaper and sets everything off to run by itself. God then remains aloof from creation and is merely a deistic theological backcloth for people, or worse, people may think God abandons creation altogether. It is necessarily difficult to recognise that the emergence of the universe and the presence of God's being are not of the same order of existence, but we believe in a missionary God whose creatorship is not just a one-off activity but a continuous activity. We could not speak of the *missio dei,* the term we use for God's mission of love to the world, unless God's creative nature were continuously present. For this reason, we also present God as the sustainer of all that is. An illustration may help here.

4.36 If a person watches a television programme, that person might well be able to describe the programme in terms of its story. A group of people watching the same programme might be able to provide a very full account, each supplying details the others had missed. In time, a very complete account might be arrived at, in correct sequential order with no gaps. But it is highly unlikely that anyone telling the story of the television programme will mention the complex array of magnets, electron guns and electronics at the back of the television set which keeps the picture continuously before our eyes when we watch the TV. Yet without these, sustaining the picture moment by moment, there would be no picture and no story. This then is how science and religion may provide complementary pictures of reality. Science deals with the story as it is oriented in linear (and asymmetric) time; Christianity emphasises that there is a creation in each and every moment, simultaneous with sustaining what is in being.

4.37

> The Big Bang theory concerns the beginning of our universe as *presently ordered*. It moves from where we are now back to the time when our universe was a very small, very dense mass. The theory does not assume that there was nothing before that small, dense mass ... even if we could identify the beginning of the universe, we would be no closer to the divine creative activity than we are right now. God's creative activity in sustaining the universe is precisely the same at the present moment as it is at every moment of the universe's existence. According to the Christian doctrine of creation, whatever exists whenever it exists owes its existence to the continuous creative activity of God. To be clear that God is the *source* of all things and that science only deals with the transformations and relations between *existing* things prevents confusions.[18]

4.38 This kind of view allows us to draw an important distinction between what theology and science are offering in answer to our questions. Under this distinction, God allows the laws of physics to be unchanging, so that the universe does conform to given, discoverable principles which scientists can describe and use in their quest for understanding.[19]

4.39 The notion that God sustains the universe and everything we can possibly know about, in being, means that Christians have something to say in any kind of debate about who and why we are. It may also give confidence to those searching for faith, that the witness of the Church can present God as the basis of our being, having been involved with every moment of our history, the history of the world and the history of the universe. Faith is not just something that fills the 'gaps' temporarily, but confirms the orderliness and sense of all creation, the very creation that God saw was 'good'.

4.40 The trouble is that some of the most important discoveries in the physical sciences can make us feel very insignificant and alone, when we try to grasp the ideas and numbers involved. For example, cosmologists can show us that the universe is about 15 billion years old and that before our evolution on earth an entire generation of stars had come into being, burned their available fuel and died, many in supernova explosions of extraordinary brightness. They can further show that *unless* a first generation of stars had died, elements such as oxygen, nitrogen, carbon and iron would not exist in the quantities needed for life to occur. We therefore seem 'fixed' in a particular age of the universe; we belong to a point in its history when it is dark and cold, and the spaces between stars so great that it seems impossible that we can reach them by our own means. In order to make sense of this, some scientists have formulated an argument called the 'anthropic principle' of which there are two forms, so-called 'weak' and 'strong'. This argument supports the view that everything scientists are discovering about the precision of quantities and balances in the universe suggests that we are meant to be here and that we are meant to observe and find out about our universe. We have a 'place' in the universe, which we can explore by means of our minds and hearts, but not, apparently, by means of hands-on experience. We cannot just go off to have a look. The distances involved are so great that even if we could travel at the speed of light many human lifetimes would pass before we could reach even the nearest stars.

4.41 This is how the poet Elizabeth Jennings feels about the realities science has discovered for us:

Delay

The radiance of the star that leans on me
Was shining years ago. The light that now
Glitters up there my eye may never see,
And so the time lag teases me with how

Love that loves now may not reach me until
Its first desire is spent. The star's impulse
Must wait for eyes to claim it beautiful
And love arrived may find us somewhere else.[20]

4.42 She touches on an important question raised by the facts of distance. When we look at the night sky we see a beautiful picture of the past. Some writers, such as Danah Zohar, also experience a sense of aloneness and isolation when confronted by these facts. Surely our little world is completely cut off? If we cannot talk directly or immediately to anyone but ourselves, how can we believe that God loves us, acts in the world, and that we are capable of transcendence? 'When I look at your heavens, the work of your fingers, the moon and the stars, that you have established; What are human beings that you are mindful of them, mortals that you care for them?' (Psalm 8.3–4).

4.43 The answer to the psalmist's cry is the other side of the poem's conclusion. That love is not of the same order as light. We can say that God loves us, because of our direct experience of that love; it is a consequence of God's missionary nature that the universe is sustained in being and permeated with the experience of God's love. We can say, further, that God's love touches every part of creation, not just human beings, and allows the universe to be in the very special and particular way that we have discovered it exists. Our journey is known, cherished and understood. The future and ultimate destiny of the universe is already mapped in God's intention, and falls into conformity with his will.

4.44 This idea that the whole of the universe's history and future is already infused with God's will helps us to make sense of what the cosmologists tell us about the fine tuning that seems to be apparent in the universe. In order for there to be observers of the universe at all, the forces of gravity and expansion at the Big Bang are reckoned to be balanced to a sensitivity of 1 in 10^{60}. This sensitivity is the same as pointing a gun at a target 1 cm^2 at the other side of the observable universe – and hitting it.[21] Now this in itself is not a proof that God did the fine tuning. If there were an infinite number of universes, it would be more than likely that one universe of this kind of sensitivity would be bound to occur sooner or later. We do not, however, have any evidence to suppose that there are any universes other than our own. What is remarkable is that it is then only in a universe of this kind that we can ourselves exist to wonder at it. We *belong* here.

4.45 What this also means is that scientists are now beginning to reassess the importance of our self-awareness, not just the fact that we are conscious, but that we are here to ask questions about the universe and discover the laws that govern it. The 'anthropic principle', as mentioned above, looks at the idea that we are somehow meant to be here.[22] Some scientists are also looking at the idea that for a universe to be, there must be conscious observers of its being, although this would be a minority speculative view. While we might claim that we know about value, purpose and meaning, we should not be sidetracked into thinking this puts us right back at the centre of the universe and that human beings are pre-eminent. As Christians we only understand value, purpose and meaning through the experience of God's love. The religious experience has the capacity to make sense of all the known details and to make our wonderings about who and why we are fall into place. This is not just an intellectual satisfaction, but a sense of wonder and awe at the intricacy of nature in all its forms.

4.46   Another manifestation of this is now given to us by chaos and complexity theory, which aims to show how small causes may have large distant effects. A now famous example is the assertion that the effect of a butterfly moving its wings in a tropical forest creates enough disturbance in the balance of the world's weather systems to effect storms in another part of the world at a later date.[23] The suggestion is that every breath we take and every motion we make is affective and interrelational. This is a holistic view of creation which science is opening up for us. But we believe the world is affective and interrelational, because this is also in the nature of God.

4.47   This is how Walt Whitman saw it:

> O vast Rondure, swimming in space,
>
> Cover'd all over with visible power and beauty,
>
> Alternate light and day and the teeming spiritual darkness,
>
> Unspeakable high processions of sun and moon and countless stars above,
>
> Below, the manifold grass and waters, animals, mountains, trees,
>
> With inscrutable purpose, some hidden prophetic intention,
>
> Now first it seems my thought begins to span thee ...
>
> After the noble inventors, after the scientists, the chemist, the geologist, ethnologist,

Finally shall come the poet worthy that name,

The true son of God shall come singing his songs.

Then not your deeds only O voyagers, O scientists and inventors, shall be justified,

All these hearts as of fretted children shall be sooth'd ...

('Passage to India', section 5)[24]

4.48 Many scientists are moved to awe and wonder by their enquiries about the universe, but such awe is commonplace among human beings. These feelings prompt us to look beyond ourselves and shake us out of our complacency. For many people, such experiences mark the beginning of a sense of transcendence and it is to these people that the witness of the Church must speak its truth. This truth will not be a counter to the experience, but will emerge from it. We therefore need to look to science to find out what can be known about the universe we contemplate and that so disturbs us. In particular, we are challenged to speak of a God who is not infinitely beyond our finite minds and unknowable, but who rather is both personal and accessible. Further, this God has revealed himself as one of us in a way that allows us to relate the human person of Jesus to the 'Cosmic Christ' of the letters to the Colossians, the Ephesians and particularly of the Prologue to St John's Gospel, who, according to the first letter of Peter, 'was destined before the foundation of the world, but was revealed at the end of the ages for your sake' (1.20).

4.49 In his book, *God in Us*,[25] the Revd Anthony Freeman, whose views are echoed by the Sea of Faith movement,[26] argued that if there is a God 'out there', we can know nothing of such a God.[27] In responding to such an idea, we can see that recent scientific thinking can help us to relate 'out there' to the entire complexity of the world in a way that is explicitly God-revealing. God is not confined within the summation of human ideals, but continuously creating and sustaining creation.

The quantum world

4.50 We are also challenged to maintain our view of such a God where scientists are probing what we can know of nature's smallest components.

Here our very notions of reality are challenged, as well as our fundamental premises about how thinking relates to experience. This is because, for any event at the quantum level, the answer you get depends on the kind of question you ask. This means that the more precisely you try to determine what has happened in one aspect of an event, the more information you lose about other aspects of it. Moreover, the very act of observation, of measurement, of human interference, itself affects what is going on. This is encapsulated in Heisenberg's Uncertainty Principle, which need not concern us here, except that there is a genuine philosophical problem about what we may and may not know located deep down at the heart of nature and with which scientists have to grapple.

4.51 Christians may have some sympathy with those scientists who are working on the indeterminism of the Uncertainty Principle, even if the way in which we approach mystery and the unknowable is a long way from the complexities of quantum physics. However, those searching for faith may well wish to know what Christians do with concepts which are outwardly unbelievable or inwardly unknowable and find reassurance from those who are familiar with both scientific and religious mystery. For example:

> If the unpicturable world of electrons gives us some surprises, we shouldn't be too amazed if the unpicturable God has some surprises in store for us also. If, as a Christian believer, I find – as I do, and as millions have done before me – that when I talk of Jesus Christ I just can't talk about him in human terms, but I'm also driven to use divine language, then I have to accept the reality of this experience, however difficult it is to understand how the infinite God and a finite man in first-century Palestine can, in some mysterious way, be joined together ... it's not a case of scientific fact versus religious opinion. It's a case, with both science and religion, of trying to interpret and understand the rich, varied and surprising way the world actually is.[28]

4.52 We are challenged to show those people who encounter the Christian faith and who simply cannot believe its message because its paradox, mystery and extraordinary claims cut against the rational, testable and measurable, that scientists too must now grapple with the strangeness and uncertainty that seem to lie at the very heart of nature.

The life sciences

EVOLUTION

- I had religious doubts from the age of about ten or eleven ... I must have been quite young, but obviously I must have been beginning to ask questions, and by the time I was thirteen or fourteen my doubts were pretty severe, and they were quite largely fuelled, I think, by evolution. I already knew about dinosaurs and about Darwin, and so on, and I think my original interest in evolution was really almost a philosophical one: how did we get here, were we really created, and ultimately, whether religion as I was taught it was true, which, by and large, I think it isn't.[29]

- Authors of the highest eminence seem to be fully satisfied with the view that each species has been independently created. To my mind it accords better with what we know of the laws impressed on matter by the Creator, that the production and extinction of the past and present inhabitants of the world should have been due to secondary causes, like those determining the birth and death of the individual. When I view all beings not as special creations, but as the lineal descendants of some few beings which lived long before the first bed of the Silurian system was deposited, they seem to me to become ennobled ... as natural selection works solely by and for the good of each being, all corporeal and mental endowments will tend to progress towards perfection.[30]

4.53 Ever since Charles Darwin wrote *The Origin of Species*, the demonstration that all life on earth, including humankind, has evolved from other creatures through time in a process of progressive and cumulative mutational change, has been perceived as a challenge to the religious understanding that God created the world and everything in it. Where the Church has failed to meet this challenge, the 'scientific' answers to the important questions have held sway. Yet this was not at all Darwin's own intention. Rather, Darwin gave a detailed insight into the nature of the created order and pronounced his own sense of wonder and amazement at the beauty and variety of the living world, of whom the Creator is the originator and under whom living things become increasingly complex and advanced.

4.54 Today, the Church is challenged by many neo-Darwinists and other evolutionary biologists whose reading of Darwin excludes the idea of origin in a Creator and any teleological function of biology. This is an important challenge, because what has not been lost in this increasingly reductionist view is a profound sense of wonder and appreciation of the variety of nature. Consequently, anyone who has been captured by the images of David Attenborough's nature films might well be convinced by Desmond Morris's argument in his wonderfully filmed television series *The Human Animal*, on the natural history of human behaviour, that religion is a behavioural response to fear of death and nothing else. Why it is that human beings alone ponder death and ultimate destiny is in itself of interest to the Church.

4.55 The Church, then, must be careful to respond to the arguments without seeking to diminish the deep love and wonder at the variety of animals and plants which biologists who attack Christian faith truly hold, for this is a point of consonance. Further, we should not, in our formation of an apologetic which answers these criticisms, forget that these scientists have a great deal to teach us, for the mission of the Church must include a comprehensive view of the integrity of creation and this is particularly something which evolutionary biology gives us.

4.56 In the rest of this section, then, we will look at the critical stance of the biologist Richard Dawkins, whose beautifully written books not only introduce his readers to the remarkable complexity of animals and plants, but also seek to refute Christian claims about the creation. These may be summarised as follows:

1. Dawkins refutes the Argument from Design as a proof of God's existence and shows it to be erroneous as a pathway to faith. In his book *Climbing Mount Improbable*,[31] he shows how complex structures such as eyes can evolve without any need for a Designer God.

2. Dawkins refutes the view that there can be any purpose to evolution. The beauty of nature is not a reflection of God's intention, but the result of the blind chance of random mutation being acted on by natural selection.[32]

3. Dawkins posits the idea of 'memes', in which ideas act like genes, ruthlessly using bodies to survive through the generations. In this argument, religious inclination or faith occurs because the 'memes' for being religiously inclined are very good at survival.

4.57 In dealing with the challenge presented by 1., the Church cannot afford to defend Paley's original argument without considering what we now know. In *Natural Theology*, William Paley argued that a stone discovered on a heath would not draw attention, but the discovery of a watch would lead the finder to infer that its existence could not be an accident and that a designer must be responsible for its existence. Extrapolating from this, he suggested that a complex organ like an eye could not have occurred through random processes and must therefore carry the evidence for God as creator. Dawkins argues that this cannot be sustained in his book *The Blind Watchmaker*.[33]

4.58 This does not, however, mean that the Christian idea of God as creator is redundant or meaningless. Richard Swinburne argues:

> God could have created humans without doing so by the long process of evolution. But that is only an objection to the theistic hypothesis if you suppose that God's only reason for creating anything is for the sake of human beings ... God also has reason to bring about animals. Animals are conscious beings who enjoy much life and perform intentional actions, even if they do not choose freely which ones to do. Of course God has a reason for giving life to elephants and giraffes, tigers and snails. And anyway the beauty of the evolution of the inanimate world from the Big Bang (or from eternity) would be quite enough of a reason for producing it, even if God were the only person to have observed it ....
>
> Darwin showed that the universe is a machine for making animals and humans. But it is misleading to gloss that correct point in the way that Richard Dawkins does ... It is misleading because it ignores the interesting question of whether the existence and operation of that machine, the factors which Darwin (and Wallace) cited to explain 'our own existence', themselves have a further explanation. I have argued that the principles of rational enquiry suggest that they do. Darwin gave a correct explanation of the existence of animals and humans; but not, I think, an ultimate one. The watch may have been made with the aid of some blind screwdrivers (or even a blind watchmaking machine), but they were guided by a watchmaker with some very clear sight.[34]

The Search for Faith

4.59 Interestingly, we can look at this idea from the point of view of Dawkins's own writing. For example, he tells us about writing a computer program to 'create' generations of insect-like pictures on the screen:

> With a wild surmise, I began to breed, generation after generation, from whatever child looked most like an insect ... I still cannot conceal from you my feeling of exultation as I first watched these exquisite creatures emerging before my eyes. I distinctly heard the triumphal opening chords of *Also sprach Zarathustra* ... in my mind, I couldn't eat, and that night 'my' insects swarmed behind my eyelids as I tried to sleep.[35]

4.60 We are called to be co-creators with God of the world which God has brought into being but which is being shaped and moulded by us. We are further to be responsible for the continuing welfare of that creation. Here Dawkins himself teaches us something of the wonder and responsibility which go with this aspect of acting in accordance with the *missio dei*. As if sensing this, Dawkins is at pains to remind us that 'his' insects, brought into being by his computer program, were not consciously created by him.[36]

4.61 Yet he continues to give us his sense of joy at perceiving the fruits of his activity, but he makes them familiar and gives them names: 'spitfire', 'scorpion', 'lunar lander'. He sees them as creatures, not just as bits of information and these accrue meaning as he labels and identifies them. He searches for them when they are 'lost' in the computer, and rejoices when he comes across some semblance of them again. He then acts (by recording their genetic codes) in order to make sure they cannot be lost any more. All of this makes sense to Christians who believe in a creator who calls individuals who become conscious of his presence by name; who searches out what is lost and rejoices in the found. These things are contained in the nature of the responsibility of creatorship, and define our own relationships to the Creator God. Dawkins therefore confirms, rather than refutes, what the mission theological view of the Creator God is. God is a creator who rejoices in our becoming, who (in existential terms) lets us be, and who waits patiently for our own wanderings to bring us at last to recognition and conformity with the excellence of the creator's originating action:

> [There is] a miraculous theophany in the stability and infinite variety of DNA .... Genetic risk is the price creation pays for the

infinite proliferation of species that grace the earth. Without such risk, life as we know it would not have been possible at all. DNA enables us to exist, systemically. As such it can declare the glory of God.[37]

4.62 What Wink says here is important for our apologetic. In his book, *River out of Eden*, Dawkins refers to a man who was converted to a deep religious faith in God by the delicate relationship between a species of orchid and the wasp which pollinates it. Dawkins shows that the relationship between wasp and orchid cannot be inferred by the Argument from Design and therefore the man's experience is based on a false premise. However, he fails to consider the actual language involved:

> I will never forget the sinking feeling that overwhelmed me, because it became clear to me in that minute that some kind of God in some kind of fashion must exist, and have an ongoing relationship with the processes by which things come into being. That in short, the creator God was not some antediluvian myth, but something real. And, most reluctantly, I also saw at once that I must search to find out more about that God.[38]

4.63 The wasp and the orchid are not the first cause of the person's disturbance (as Dawkins assumes). Rather, these form the *agency* by which the person is stimulated to think about God. Although the wonder that the person feels is not clarified by the arguments concerning cumulative evolution, that person's being is profoundly stirred and the need for enquiry kindled. Dawkins's arguments against the validity of this experience cannot preclude the possibility that God may indeed act in this way to disturb individuals.

4.64 This example similarly helps us with Dawkins's argument against teleological principles being effective in nature. As an evolutionary biologist, Dawkins can show that there are as many evolutionary dead ends and extinctions as there are surviving species and flourishing phenotypes. He is especially helpful in showing how evolutionary stable societies (a theory developed by Maynard Smith above) develop genetically.

4.65 As Christians we hold that purpose does obtain in the created world in the sense that we believe in a kingdom theology which represents a cumulative process of corporate human interaction towards a different kind of stable society, which will be realised eschatologically. Inevitably, we tend to stray from this ideal, although our own working, as Christians, is for conformity with God's intention as we understand it, such as the vision which is given to us in Isaiah 65:

> For I am about to create new heavens and a new earth;
>
> the former things shall not be remembered or come to mind.
>
> But be glad and rejoice forever in what I am creating;
>
> for I am about to create Jerusalem as a joy and its people as a delight.
>
> I will rejoice in Jerusalem, and delight in my people;
>
> No more shall the sound of weeping be heard in it or the cry of distress.
>
> No more shall there be in it an infant that lives but a few days,
>
> or an old person who does not live out a lifetime ...
>
> They shall build houses and inhabit them; they shall plant vineyards and eat their fruit.
>
> They shall not build and another inhabit; they shall not plant and another eat;
>
> for like the days of a tree shall the days of my people be,
>
> and my chosen shall long enjoy the work of their hands.
>
> They shall not labour in vain, or bear children for calamity;
>
> for they shall be offspring blessed by the Lord
>
> and their descendants as well.
>
> Before they call I will answer, while they are yet speaking I will hear.
>
> The wolf and the lamb shall feed together, the lion shall eat straw like the ox.

4.66 In this way, then, what biologists tell us about behaviour and genetic influence makes sense in terms of what we are trying to achieve through our own generations in accordance (we believe) with God's will.[39] It is interesting that Dawkins is very unhappy with 'Why?' questions and attempts to bypass these as irrelevant (this is a true test of reductionism). For him the world, as it is, is so intricate and extraordinary that it is almost sacrilegious (this word advisedly) to place it in a larger context.[40]

4.67 We can further see that, in the attempt to reduce religious belief to a marginal quirk, some life scientists then try to provide descriptions of all parts of life, even moral choices and religious understanding, in their own terms. Richard Dawkins has proposed that religion may be the result of a kind of mental virus ('memes') which infects successive generations, replicating itself purposelessly across generations. The Christian response to the idea of 'memes' includes the charge that it is not serious science and that it is merely elaborate argument to make all nature subscribe to the selfish gene theory.[41] To those searching for faith, the idea may come across that belief is merely an intellectual construct arising from inherited memes; the relationism of Christian encounter with a personal God is simply absent.

4.68 Dawkins also discusses altruistic behaviour in terms of gene strategy and shows interesting evidence for it, but others, such as Lyall Watson, extrapolating from Dawkins, are able to propose an 'anthropology of evil', as for example in *Dark Nature*,[42] in which Watson seeks to redefine good and evil in biological terms by drawing freely from other scientific disciplines. We therefore have to be critical of pseudoscience creeping in on the back of the scientific frame of reference (such as Darwinism) which makes sweeping statements aimed at excluding theology from those areas where people may find the Christian perspective most helpful.[43] Notions of repentance, conversion, forgiveness, judgement, mercy and the giving of peace are strongly operative in the gospel message and these must not be undermined by uncritical scientific views which suggest that we are driven to act solely by our genes.

4.69 This is related to the response we must make to those reductionist scientists, such as Francis Crick (who discovered the structure of DNA), in *The Astonishing Hypothesis*, who claims that human beings are no more than their neurological processes. What we pass on in the process of evangelisation is not a package of information *per se*, but a life-transforming experience which is taken over and made relevant in the context of another person's life. Persons who have almost no mind can therefore also witness to being touched by God in a meaningful and transformative way. To this extent, Christians know that conscious experience and experience of personality are additional to what is going on in the brain. For this reason, the mentally disabled and the terminally ill are still to be valued as human beings loved by God, and capable of contributing to the Christian community. Similarly, there are traditions in the Christian Church which see it meaningful to include the dead in remembrance and prayer in a way which is thought to enrich the spiritual life of the living. In evolutionary biology, the dead have no purpose except in terms of the legacy of genes. In Christian understanding, the dying and the dead form part of the community of faith which generates hope in the kingdom and the *eschaton*.

4.70 Another telling example of how much further our Christian hope extends is given in this extract. An explorer from Oxford has a theological conversation with his indigenous guide:

> 'At Kapit, I reach the fifth grade. We taught to be Christian at school. The old men they think like that. They believe in the spirits. Me and Inghai, sometimes they think they right, sometimes we laugh at them. What about you, Redmon? Do you believe it?'
>
> 'No, I don't. But I don't believe in Christianity, either. I think that when we die, we rot. And that's the end of it.'
>
> 'Then I very sorries for you,' said Leon, looking immeasurably sad, getting up and collecting his things. 'I tired, I sleep now.'[44]

4.71 In this story, Leon feels that Redmond is deeply lacking a part of his essential self, and regrets Redmond's reductionist view of his ultimate destiny. It is this basic understanding that we are more than the sum of our parts that makes sense of the Christian conviction that religious faith is more than the influence of 'memes'. In this sense, then, we are able to refute the reductionist view and seek to assert that the experience of the life scientists feeds into, rather than destroys, our view of the world.

4.72 There is one further problem which Christians must address, both from the point of view of reductionism and of modern technology. In the field of enquiry known as Strong AI (Artificial Intelligence), the study of the capabilities of computers, human beings are not an end point in evolution, but a means to the equipping of supercomputers. This kind of suggestion again moves away from the centrality of humans in the narrative of existence. In *The Dragons of Eden*,[45] the astronomer Carl Sagan suggests that computers are 'intended' to travel through space and colonise other planets, carrying our acquired wisdom and (if we insist on being anthropocentric), our genes and memes. Again, this is a speculative inference from what we know about computers, but even the idea confronts the religious notion of a special and privileged relationship with a Creator God who created us in his image.

4.73 Further, a God who becomes a human being is missing the point if human beings are only an intermediate stage in cosmic history. This means that Christian apologetics must move beyond the argument for God as Mind, which may for many of those searching for faith be seen as unhelpful.[46] God's action in and among human beings is personal and involves not just mind but body as well. This is borne out through the Incarnation of the eternal Word as Jesus and only makes sense in the totality of what we are. Our theology of kingdom and resurrection is based on fulfilment of our human potential: 'yet in our flesh shall we see God'. Our creatureliness is therefore an integral part of this vision and not negotiable with Sagan's version of Strong AI.

4.74 If we separate out scientific knowledge and speculation we can say that as science continues to advance into unknown areas, it will not push God further and further back into the dark spaces, but reveal God as intricately bound up with all that is, has been and will be. If God guarantees the laws of physics, sustains the quarks and gluons, then God is present in singularities and black holes and in adenine, guanine, cytosine and thymine, the building blocks of DNA. Everything we explore and seek to know can become a potential agent of revelation, mediated to us through our explorations, if only we do not lose sight of the religious perspective that informs the world with meaning and hold on to our faith as providing a complementary and significant insight into the results of scientific enquiry.

Technology and ethics

4.75 One further aspect of the relationship between science and religious faith raises an important challenge for the Christian Church. Because technology is so advanced and its mechanism so specialised that only those specially trained are likely to understand it, this means that many people may have to make decisions which are increasingly complex about how their lives are affected by technology. The area in which this becomes acute is that of medicine, where people may be baffled by the kinds of choices they have to make and need help in making (literally) life and death decisions. It is therefore a challenge to the mission of the Church that it should be equipped to stand alongside people as they make their way through moral labyrinths in order to allow them to make choices which include their search for faith, or their own spiritual journey. We may say that any such complex decision has a spiritual dimension, and that the decision made, whatever it is, affects a person's relationship with God. The Church is able to empathise with the difficulty of decisions and painful choices and should not be afraid to promote a vision of the kingdom through the complex ethics of decision-making.

4.76 For example, medical technology can alleviate problems of infertility. *In vitro* fertilisation (IVF), the use of donor gametes, and surrogacy arrangements may give joy and hope to some childless couples but also bring the need to face new decisions. Most of the techniques involved give rise to questions of ethical complexity. What may be the effects on a couple of introducing sperm or ova from another party in order to make it possible for them to have a child? In IVF, more embryos are produced than is required for implantation into the mother's womb. What should happen to these so-called 'spare' embryos? Is it permissible to use them for experimental purposes, perhaps to further research into the causes of genetic disease or miscarriage? To whom do they belong if the parents die? People entering IVF may be buoyed up by hope of a family, but bewildered by the choices that they alone must make in the process of achieving it.[47] There are ontological questions involved, for what is the status of a frozen embryo or frozen eggs or sperm?[48]

4.77 For some people, these technologies may appear to represent a way of safeguarding and controlling an otherwise hazardous and uncertain future, irrespective of the complex issues involved. At the extreme end of this perspective, there are those who desire their bodies cryogenically frozen in the hope of a resurrection to earthly life via technology, like the *Cold Lazarus* of Dennis Potter's final work.

4.78 Testing for genetic diseases also presses difficult choices on people. It is possible for embryos to be screened before implantation for an expanding number of conditions. Should an embryo carrying a gene which predisposes towards the onset of cancer in early adulthood not be implanted in the mother? Again, there is a difficulty in making a decision for a future that is unknown. How do couples weigh the decision whether to choose abortion for a foetus shown to carry a disease gene against the levels of suffering likely to be experienced by the child and the ability of parents to care for that child? A recent case of a mother's distress at the abortion of a healthy foetus, whom she believed to have Down's Syndrome, highlights the problems of placing one's faith exclusively in technology. How does the child of an adult whose genetic disease reveals itself late in life decide whether they themselves should be tested to see if they carry the disease gene?

4.79 Technology also raises questions about the quality of life available to people. Although technology may prevent death, its application can, in some instances, leave people with severe impairment. How do patients, doctors and relatives make decisions about whether treatment should be pursued at all costs? How can doctors be supported in situations where technology has to be rationed between patients? A related example is provided by the decision where some people raise huge sums of money to send the desperately ill to other centres in the hope of finding a technology which will provide the cure. Not only do they risk using up what time they have left with the loved one in pursuit of this ambition, they also face increased pain if their efforts are in vain. There are difficult decisions facing families who are asked to consent to switching of life support machines and who ask that their loved ones be allowed to die.[49] This is not to say that such people should not act in this faith, but surely those who place it in technology should be offered something more through the Church's witness, if technology lets them down? At the same time, we should not forget the witness of the doctors who, together with hospital chaplains, also have an important role in the recognition of, and alleviation of, spiritual pain:

> Doctors need increasingly to be aware of these issues, to have thought out their own beliefs and to be able, sensitively, to offer spiritual help if this is asked for. They should be aware of the patient's religious belief so that the specific practices of the Christian, Jew, Moslem, Hindu, or Buddhist can be adhered to.[50]

4.80 At the other end of the spectrum from IVF, people may be faced with difficult choices arising from technological ability to keep people alive. Discussion about PVS (Persistent Vegetative State) as highlighted by the Tony Bland case, has recently come back into focus following some reported recoveries from this apparently hopeless condition. There are many stories about the dilemma of families faced with switching off a life support machine, or agreeing to organ donation, but these stories point particularly to the need of the Church to provide a story about life and death which can make sense of the decisions which people make, *whichever way they make them*. What we are saying here is that the mission of the Church is not served exclusively by the application of Christian ethics, which may perhaps untangle what it is needed to do, but by providing a larger context in which any kind of difficult decision may be offered into God's future.[51] Perhaps the most helpful way of describing this is by former Archbishop Runcie's words at Helen House, the hospice for children with life-threatening illnesses in Oxford: 'No life, however short, is ever wasted; ... no life in which love has been given and received is anything other than complete.'[52] This perspective allows the anguish of intensely difficult decisions to be balanced against the importance of memory and relationships, and of the gaining of a future which is not uncertain, but already prepared and in which all tears will be wiped away.

Summary

KEY WORDS

- myth ● creed ● science ● choice ● complementarity
- whole person ● purpose ● value ● meaning ● God-of-the-gaps ● God as sustainer ● evolution ● genes ● ethics

Questions about the world and about ourselves may often lead to a perception that science and religious belief, including Christianity, provide frames of reference which are very different, if not mutually exclusive. The Christian frame of reference is provided by the creed, but where people encounter this later rather than sooner, they may find it hard to map on to the way Christian belief makes sense of the world. For some people, science can displace, disprove, or explain away religious understanding and experience, or marginalise religious truth altogether. People may feel the need to choose between scientific and religious frames of reference, and not realise the possibilities for complementarity. It may be necessary to look towards an holistic approach to which both scientific and religious perspectives contribute. This may be especially true in healing issues. Christians have a way of thinking which generates hope, a way of understanding that is personal and relevant and a way of describing reality in terms of value, purpose and meaning.

The discoveries in the natural sciences may lead to a defensive God-in-the-gaps theology, but God can be seen as the sustainer of all, including the laws of science. The 'anthropic principle' asks us to look again at what we think is our place in the universe. Chaos and complexity theory asks us to look for a new set of relationships between cause and effect in the world we know.

The Church is also challenged by theories of evolution and by reductionist tendencies among some life scientists. The Church can respond in seeing nature as an agency for discovering God and in rediscovering teleological principles. The way in which the Church thinks about life after death also challenges the view that we are only vehicles for our selfish genes.

We also have to deal with the role and purpose of computer technology and with the status of human beings in a computer-controlled world. We may see that computers are but one manifestation of complex technologies which may be used by people every day without their understanding how they function. People are sometimes faced by complex ethical decisions, especially in situations where life and death are surrounded by medical technology. It is important for the Church's witness that Christians stand alongside those who have to make such decisions.

Further reading

Appleyard, Bryan, *Understanding the Present: Science and the Soul of Modern Man*, Pan, 1992.

Dawkins, Richard, *The Blind Watchmaker*, Penguin edition, 1988.

Hawking, Stephen, *A Brief History of Time*, Bantam Press, 1988.

Montefiore, Hugh, *Credible Christianity: The Gospel in Contemporary Society*, Mowbray, 1993.

Polkinghorne, John, *Quarks, Chaos and Christianity*, Triangle, 1994.

Swinburne, Richard, *Is There A God?*, OUP, 1996.

Wijngaards, John, *Making Sense of God*, Sheed and Ward/Housetop, 1995.

The Search for Faith

Things to do

- **AIM:** to become less defensive about Christianity in the face of scientific advances.
- **PURPOSE:** to find ways to allow people to make Christian faith prominent in dealing with science and technology.

BIBLE VERSE

> Do you know the ordinances of the heavens? Can you establish their rule on the earth? (Job 38.33)

Things to do include:

a. Thinking about household items
b. Drawing imaginary animals
c. Discussing hospital treatment
d. Discussion questions

E. HOUSEHOLD ITEMS

Ask people in small groups to make a list of common household objects and appliances (you could use pictures from magazines or catalogues) and discuss:

- whether you could mend it if it broke
- whether you could do without it (and if not, why not)
- what the level of inconvenience without it would be.

Then consider:

- what life would be like without God
- whether you could do without God
- what you would do if you suddenly lost your faith.

2. IMAGINARY ANIMALS

Ask one pair of people to be judges. Ask people singly or in pairs to describe or to draw an imaginary animal or plant which is not like any other. If people can be encouraged to spend time doing this beforehand this may help the exercise.

Ask the judges to decide which are the best three animals. All the others are deemed extinct.

Now ask the 'creators' of the winners to say what their animals are 'for' and why they should survive. Ask the judges to decide which animal gets to rule the world.

Now discuss how people felt about the exercise. Did it matter if your animal died out? Did this exercise help at all in understanding how God relates to creation? Would you prefer it if you had lost your animal by blind chance?

3. OPERATIONS

Ask which members of the group have had an operation, or other hospital treatment, or had babies in hospital. Group people as far as possible with similar experiences. All others can go in a 'dentist's chair group'!

Ask the groups to talk about their feelings with respect to:
- what was happening to them
- the doctors and nurses
- the pain
- the machines and instruments.

Did this experience make you think about faith in God?

4. DISCUSSION QUESTIONS

Choose such questions as may be relevant to your group.

a. Does our belief offer anything to people which science does not?
b. Are we wrong to say we have a privileged place in the universe?
c. What place have awe and wonder in religion and science?
d. Is the future only as good as our computers?
e. Is the Church guilty of creating a God-of-the-gaps?

f. Do the theories of evolution and the creation stories in Genesis mean that we have to abandon one or the other?
g. How do we help those making difficult decisions relating to medical technology?
h. Should schools teach scientific and religious views about the world at the same time?

Notes

1. Quoted as the beginning of a preface to *Subtle is the Lord ... The Science and the Life of Albert Einstein*, by Abraham Pais, OUP, 1982.
2. Stephen Hawking, *A Brief History of Time*, Bantam Press, 1988, p.122.
3. From Craig Raine, 'Listen with Mother' in *A Martian Sends a Postcard Home*, OUP, 1979, p.3.
4. See Hawking, op. cit., p.141.
5. Oliver Sacks, *Migraine: Understanding the Common Disorder*, University of California Press, 1985, Pan edition, pp.106–9.
6. For example, in *The Periodic Kingdom*, Basic Books, HarperCollins, Weidenfield and Nicholson 1995, Peter Atkins lays out the patterns underlying the table of chemical elements and shows how the missing elements, not naturally occurring in nature, can be created (if practicable) by human beings. All 'gaps' can be filled in by human reason.
7. For example, the Revd Dr John Polkinghorne at Cambridge in e.g. *Science and Christian Belief: Theological Reflections of a Bottom-up Thinker*, SPCK, 1994, and the Revd Dr Arthur Peacocke at Oxford in e.g. *Theology for a Scientific Age*, Blackwell, 1990.
8. See Lewis Wolpert and Alison Richards, *A Passion for Science*, OUP, 1988, p.22.
9. Hugh Montefiore, *Credible Christianity: The Gospel in Contemporary Society*, Mowbray, 1993, p.18.
10. See Paul Davies, *God and the New Physics*, Penguin edition, 1990, p.229. Also see *The Mind of God*, Penguin edition, 1993.
11. In Thomas Hardy's *The Return of the Native*, the remedy for Mrs Yeobright's adder bite is reckoned to be rubbing the wound with the fat of fried adders.
12. *Four Quartets*, East Coker IV.
13. Jeremy Woodcock, 'Refugees and Western Sensibilities', in *The Way*, Vol. 36, January 1996, No. 1, p.13. Also see Anne Nasimiyu-Wasike, 'Christology and an African Woman's experience' in Robert Schreiter (ed.), *Faces of Jesus in Africa*, SCM, 1992.
14. The Revd Dr T. Mervyn Willshaw, *What on Earth is God Doing?*, paper to the Methodist Apologetics Group, 3 April 1995, pp.6, 10.

15. For example, see Pietro Redondi, *Galileo: Heretic*, translated by Raymond Rosenthal, Penguin edition, 1989. Also see J. H. Brooke, *Science and Religion*, CUP, 1991.
16. This example is taken from a talk given by the Revd Dr David Wilkinson entitled 'Spirituality and Modern Cosmology' given to the Alister Hardy Research Centre London Group on 13 September 1994.
17. Hawking, op. cit., pp.140–41.
18. Diogenes Allen, *Christian Belief in a Post-Modern World*, Westminster/John Knox Press, 1989, pp.47–8.
19. The illustration from Dr David Wilkinson, op. cit.
20. Elizabeth Jennings, 'Delay' in *Collected Poems*, Carcanet, 1986, p.15.
21. See Paul Davies, *God and the New Physics*, Penguin edition, 1990, p.179.
22. See, for example, John D. Barrow and Frank J. Tipler, *The Anthropic Cosmological Principle*, OUP, 1986, or John Leslie, *Universes*, Routledge, 1989.
23. For example, see John Polkinghorne, *Quarks, Chaos and Christianity*, Triangle, 1994, p.57.
24. Walt Whitman, *Leaves of Grass*, Airmont edition, 1965, pp.287–8.
25. *God in Us*, SCM, 1993.
26. This movement takes its name from Matthew Arnold's poem 'Dover Beach':
    The sea of faith
        was once, too, at the full, and round earth's shore
    Lay like the folds of a bright girdle furl'd;
    But now I only hear
        Its melancholy, long, withdrawing roar,
    Retreating to the breath
        Of the nightwind down the vast edges drear
    And naked shingles of the world.
27. The Bishop of Oxford, the Rt Revd Richard Harries engaged Anthony Freeman in a public debate on the issue and his response is contained in *The Real God*, Mowbray, 1994.
28. John Polkinghorne, op. cit., p.17.
29. John Maynard Smith, 'Making it Formal', in Lewis Wolpert and Alison Richards, op. cit., p.129.
30. Charles Darwin, *The Origin of Species*, Penguin edition, 1968, pp.458–9.
31. *Climbing Mount Improbable*, Viking, 1996.
32. Here, the Church has the opportunity to uphold the transcendental basis for the apprehension of and appreciation of beauty, and theories of aesthetics.
33. Richard Dawkins, *The Blind Watchmaker*, Penguin edition, 1988, see chapter 1, 'Explaining the Very Improbable', pp.1–18.
34. Richard Swinburne, *Is There A God?*, OUP, 1996, pp.62–3.
35. Dawkins, op. cit., pp.59–60.
36. Ibid. See pp.63–4.

37. Walter Wink, *Unmasking the Powers*, Fortress Press, 1986, p.147.
38. Richard Dawkins, *River out of Eden*, HarperCollins Science Masters, 1995, p.60.
39. See another view of the role of God in evolution in John Wijngaards' argument about God's creative energy and the emergence of 'face' in *Making Sense of God*, Sheed and Ward/Housetop, 1995, pp.178–9.
40. See *River out of Eden*, chapter 4, 'God's Utility Function'.
41. J. Bowker, *Is God a Virus?*, SPCK, 1995 is a Christian response to Dawkins's 'memes'.
42. And see Timothy Anders, *The Evolution of Evil*, Open Court, 1994.
43. See, for example, Philip Hefner, *The Human Factor*, Fortress Press, 1993.
44. Redmond O'Hanlon, *Into the Heart of Borneo*, Penguin edition, 1985, p.122.
45. Hodder and Stoughton, 1977.
46. See 'God as Cosmic Mind' in John Wijngaards, op. cit.
47. See *Choices in Childlessness*, Free Church Federal Council/British Council of Churches, 1982.
48. See, for example, *Personal Origins*, Church House Publishing, 1985, revised 1996.
49. See *Euthanasia – No!*, a joint submission by the House of Bishops of the Church of England and the Catholic Bishops' Conference of England and Wales to the House of Lords Select Committee on Medical Ethics, Catholic Truth Society, 1993.
50. M. J. Baines, 'Terminal Illness' in D. J. Weatherall, J. G. G. Ledingham and D. A. Warrell (eds), *Oxford Textbook of Medicine*, third edition, OUP, 1996, p.4359.
51. See Kevin T. Kelly, *Life and Love: Towards a Christian Dialogue on Bioethical Questions*, Collins, 1987.
52. Quoted in David Atkinson, *Jesus, Lamb of God: Biblical Meditations*, SPCK, 1996, pp.11–12.

5

From Lamb of God to dead sheep

I won't tell you my name. I experience the world as a dead, dark place. The Christian Gospel is just a system of ideas which have been passed around for centuries. Half those Christians couldn't agree with the other half most of the time – so much for 'truth'. What's that supposed to say to people in this crazy, broken world? Anyway, the Church hasn't got anything relevant to say to people like me nowadays: to women, for instance, or gay people. What's more, it doesn't adapt to the way we have to live these days; it doesn't accommodate what we're capable of. What does the Church have to say about the Holocaust, tell me that?

Christians should put up or shut up. Except that they haven't got anything to put up. So just what are you going to do about it?

Introduction

Where do our ideas in western society actually come from? Are people free to formulate their own mental worlds? Are we the inheritors of thinking traditions, or are we, and they, conditioned by the kind of society we live in?

This chapter examines the history of ideas, looking at the way our own modes of thinking about God have changed over the centuries. What does Christian theology, including mission theology, look like today, and has it got any real relevance in contemporary society?

We can see, by examining the history of ideas, that the Christian message has been challenged and affected by other ways of thinking about the world and the relationship between human beings and God. In particular, theological thinking has been especially challenged by ideas which provide satisfactory explanations of the way the world is and the place of humanity in it, so that there seems to be no point bringing God into it at all. Where God has apparently been pushed into the background, it is up to the Church to form an apologetic that helps people to see that human ideas are but an approach to the overarching knowledge which God has of us.

The Search for Faith

As we approach the twenty-first century, it is up to us to find ways of showing that the promises of the Christian Gospel bring meaning, purpose and hope into experiences in human life where there seems nothing left to say.

The history of ideas

Where we're at

5.1 Damien Hirst, the artist, who drew attention with his *Dead Sheep*, recently won the Turner Prize for Art 1995 with his exhibit *Cow and Calf* at the Tate Gallery. This consisted of the two animals, each cut in half and preserved in their separate halves in four glass cases. The viewer perceives the deadness of the suspended animals, little bubbles clinging to their fur; meaningless viscera; the separation of mother and progeny and self from self. Hirst refuses connections even with natural processes, for the animals cannot even decompose naturally. The viewer may end up outraged, inspired, bewildered, sad ...

5.2 In a way, this prize-winning exhibit is a good mirror of the so-called post-modern culture in which we live. We cannot say what *Cow and Calf* means – it might be meaningless, no more than two dead animals in four pieces in a room. We have to create meanings. It is possible to walk between the two halves of the animals and look at their insides, but effectively learn very little; observers cannot examine or test the viscera. Everything is walled off: the attendant will not allow touching or leaning on the glass. If there is a message, it is one of fragmentation, one of inability for reconstruction. If a theologically minded observer were to ask 'Where is God?', the answer would probably be 'Not here'. For as the Roman Catholic artist and writer David Jones wrote: 'I have felt for His Wounds/in nozzles and containers .... A, a, a, Domine Deus, my hands found the glazed work unrefined and the terrible crystal a stage-paste.'[1]

5.3 Some of the other artists in the Turner Prize exhibition offered canvases created by dripping turpentine on to painted backgrounds; empty cages illuminated by a single suspended light (do not touch) and a continuous videotape of the interior of the artist's body via an endoscope.

5.4   We may well sympathise if people are bored, irritated or mystified by rooms full of bricks, rice or dead animals, even more when such art wins prizes and is highly valued. But perhaps such exhibits are really worth this price, where they reflect accurately the nature of our western culture, and where material worth is the touchstone of validity or 'realness'. It is uncomfortable and disturbing to look at images which sum up the way we are all required to live if we participate in society. Peter Greenaway, the film director, as interested as Hirst in death (but also in decomposition) is pleased with the description of his work as bright painted butterflies, held down by brass pins: a drawerful of dead exhibits.[2] His films, such as *A Zed and Two Noughts*, *The Belly of an Architect*, *The Thief, the Cook, his Wife and her Lover* and *Prospero's Books*, occupy themselves with showing how the bright, sophisticated exteriors of human society conceal rottenness and decay, a world in which human beings eat each other: the inside of the cow.

5.5   Immediately, we are faced with a crucial question: how can the Christian Church act in *mission* in such an environment? For what we are seeing and the tools we are given for sense-making include refusal of privileged position, separation and estrangement, a kaleidoscope of fragments. Is there anything to say? And if there is, and we say it, how can it be received by people whose lives are conditioned by threading their way through a pick'n'mix society? How can we uphold the story of the Lamb of God in the culture of modern western society where a vision of artistic excellence is a dead sheep?

5.6   The Church of England's General Synod Board of Education has helpfully provided a broader description of post-modernism:

> The world acts in a post-modern way when
>
> it 'picks'n'mixes'
>
> it is laid back and playful
>
> it distrusts logic and rationality,
>
> it is suspicious of history and tradition
>
> it distrusts the idea of progress
>
> it likes fuzzy boundaries
>
> it refuses to judge

> Its critics would say that in a post-modern world
> 'pick'n'mix' avoids the difficult and disquieting
> babble replaces discourse and dialogue
> pools of ignorance replace founts of knowledge
> everything is good for a laugh
> the coinage of qualifications is debased
> opinion passes for truth[3]

5.7 If, then, we live in a world of babble, opinion and pools of ignorance, we can see that we may be in danger of losing that which is essential to the mission of the Church. If generations go by who have not heard the gospel, or who lose it in the babble, and if Christian witness is seen as another option among many and if the contiguity of Christian lives is ruptured by capriciousness, how shall they (and we) hear?

5.8 In his book *After Virtue*,[4] Alasdair MacIntyre begins by proposing that if everything we know about science were to be destroyed and fragmented and then put back together, we could only have a very partial and distorted view of what science was once like. His imaginary scenario is similar to some contemporary visions of what human society might be like after a nuclear holocaust if all our technology were destroyed. A great deal of information would have been lost and might possibly be irreplaceable. His vision is also complicated by his contention that if such a scenario came about we would not be able to diagnose what was actually wrong, because such a synchronic view would not supply the relevant information. For this reason he argues for a <u>diachronic, historical overview which provides a context</u> for seeing where we are, for locating ourselves.

5.9 In this chapter we shall adopt MacIntyre's suggestion, for if we are to respond with a mission strategy for our times, we need to see how we have arrived at this kind of culture and to see how the Church has responded in the past to challenges from western culture. In a chapter like this, it is not possible to spend a large amount of time discussing the complexities of the various movements and history of ideas.[5] It will be our aim merely to give a general outline and some illustration of the way we have inherited the various systems of thought in our own time. Furthermore, when we consider the search for faith and the witness of the Church, we have to ask whether those who search for faith are accustomed to thinking and rationalising in ways which do not, in fact, make reception of the gospel an easy task.

5.10 In the spirit of post-modern playfulness and as an analogy we may consider our method to be like a journey, passing through strategic points, but not stopping to explore every detail of the new place. We shall also concentrate on three of the various forms of ambush, all of which have particular consequences in the twentieth century:

- the challenge of 'heretical' thinking
- the 'triumph' of human reason
- the threat of death and silence

Where we're coming from: the development of Christian thought in the west

> Philosophy
> is a walk on the slippery rocks
> Religion
> is a light in the fog
>
> (Edie Brickell and the New Bohemians, 'What I Am', The David Geffen Company, 1988)

5.11 As Christians interested in mission, we might account for ourselves as follows:

The significance of what God has done for human beings, in creation, in salvation history and supremely in giving his Son Jesus Christ, is too great to be comprehended in its entirety. For the story is complete, but not ended; the history of Christianity has continued and is continuing under the guidance of the Holy Spirit towards the establishment of God's reign and a time when there is not anything that does not point directly to God: that theophany of the New Jerusalem that we call the *eschaton*. Christians act in mission both individually and as the Body of Christ precisely because the story is not ended, for we understand it to be part of God's purposes to include all human beings and all of creation in the ultimate story.

How is it that we might come to make such a statement?

5.12 The theology which informs Christian teaching and our understanding of mission has grown up out of a grounding in Scripture and tradition. These are our own primary narratives, the stories we live by, but we do not inherit *just* a story, or a collection of ideas. We also inherit the experience of Christian people living Christian lives whose faith becomes part of our heritage and collective cultural memory. It is perhaps useful to remember that all theologians are human beings whose thinking is subject to their worldview and temperament. Further, when Christianity began to spread from its point of origin throughout the world, it had the property not just of presenting a system of ideas, but a way of being that was transformative. It became embedded in the culture of peoples, overriding or absorbing old ways and old beliefs. This means that we have to consider two strands when we look at the history of ideas: the development of thinking and the development of culture. When we act in mission we also appeal to people to think about themselves and God, and we relate the story of God's saving acts to the experience of being in the world and participating in it. The correlation of the two is supported by our witness: we are Christians and our lives are examples, no matter what Christian denomination we belong to.

Heresy: the grit in the oyster?

5.13 First then, we may begin our journey through the first millennium and visit the places where believers tried to clarify what God had actually done in Jesus Christ. And here, we must consider the role of heresy (or 'alternative' Christian teaching) as driving the need to define the content of Christian orthodoxy. There are two ways in which we can think about heresy. The first is that alternative ideas about what God has done and is doing arise to challenge neglect of aspects of the faith. In early times, this sometimes happened as a consequence of a political or power struggle, but also meant that dialogue, resulting in redefinition of belief, made sure that Christianity did not stagnate. Because of a continuing dialectic, our understanding of Christianity has accumulated. This is fundamentally important to mission, for as we explore more ways of understanding God's story, so the missionary task becomes better described. Today, for example, the contribution of liberation theologies[6] and, in particular, Third World theologies challenges us in the west not to be complacent about what we think we know about God. It is most often a fresh perspective arising from different contexts, or outwardly an alternative or complementary view which can become the prophetic word.

5.14 The second way in which we need to talk about heresy is where it becomes the label attached to distortions of the Christian faith which need to be identified and exposed. The importance of dealing with heretical ideas is made clear to us in studies such as C. FitzSimons Allison's book *The Cruelty of Heresy*, where he tries to show that it is a human trait to try to adapt God's truth to our own ends and that this happens in every age, including our own, so that:

> We are susceptible to heretical trends because, in one form or another, they nurture and reflect the way we would have it be rather than the way God has provided, which is infinitely better for us. As they lead us into the blind alleys of self-indulgence and escape from life, heresies pander to the most unworthy tendencies of the human heart.[7]

5.15 He reminds us that it is our task in mission to point up 'the way God has provided' and to show the deficiency of readings of the gospel which suit only the devices and desires of our own hearts. 'As we hear and retell the gospel, we unwittingly distort the story, thus reinforcing any heresy of which we may be a victim.'[8] Allison therefore suggests that we cannot form a response without self-examination and this is as true today as it was in the early centuries of Christian thought. We need to keep these two rather different perspectives on 'heresy' in mind, as we continue on our journey.

5.16 In the early Church, orthodoxy was honed against other teachings concerning who God is and who Jesus is. Docetism said that Jesus had only one, divine nature; Ebionism suggested the opposite: that Jesus had only one, human nature. Neither of these views made sense of the resurrection of Jesus as occasioning the salvation of humankind. If 'the way God has provided' for us was to be upheld, then Jesus had to have had two natures: being fully human and fully divine. This recognition underpins the words of Athanasius: 'God became man that man might become God.' This statement has important consequences for mission theology, for the notion that God's action in giving us his son Jesus Christ is to effect an ultimate act of becoming underpins the whole reason for witness and proclamation of the gospel.

5.17   As Christian theology developed, so did the notion of Trinitarianism. The Council of Nicaea, reacting against the teachings of Arius (c. 256–336), determined that Jesus was of one being with the Father, of the same substance (*homoousios*) and not of merely *like* substance (*homoiousios*), and therefore that being-in-relation was a characteristic of God. Being and being-in-relation became seen as the twin touchstones for existence. This was not just a matter of intellectual discussion in a vacuum, but borne out by the experience of the Christian community's own fellowship (*koinonia*). Being a Christian, then, is not just about adopting a set of beliefs, but about being in relationship with other Christians. Moreover, this fellowship is not just that of human relations, but is allied to our participation in the divine life. This divine life is described as being in (or as) communion where the persons of the Trinity exist as an interpenetration *(perichoresis)* of mutuality and love, such that it is not possible to speak of the Father without simultaneously referring to the Son and to the Holy Spirit: one being (*ousia*) in three persons (*hypostases*).[9]

5.18   The great Councils of the early Christian Church, at Nicaea (325), at Constantinople (381), and at Ephesus (431); St Augustine (354–430) in the west, together with the triad of fourth-century thinkers, Basil of Caesarea (330–379), Gregory of Nazianus (329–389) and Gregory of Nyssa (d. c. 394) in the east, all helped to establish the critical doctrines which underlie the description of God as a sending, or missionary God, experienced in history by human beings: 'the more explicit creeds of the fourth century helped to mark the boundaries and limits of what we can authentically teach about God who is Father, Son and Holy Spirit, without sacrificing something of the redemptive experience of Christians.'[10] The rejection by the eastern churches of an added phrase in the creed that says that the Holy Spirit proceeds from the Father and the Son *(filioque* clause) has meant that some issues remain open and worthy of exploration and ecumenical discussion right up to the present day.[11]

5.19   We can see, then, that the establishment of the Canon of Scripture, the development of the creeds, the decisions about the nature of Jesus's being and the resolution of the discussion concerning the Trinity, brought into existence the tools for mission in and to the world. But we may also see that these would be challenged by ways of thinking which privileged the holder of alternative ideas. Consequently, the Church has not always held the same views about everything continuously, as Professor Paul Badham has pointed out.[12] Rather, the Church has had to move forward on the basis of aggregated knowledge, culled on the experience of being Christian and from the continuous debate about Christian belief. What we must also understand is that 'heresy' is not just a thought-system but a way of behaving and so its characteristics, which challenge the historic faith, may appear at other times and places.[13] For example:

> Concrete situations of diapers, debts, divorce or listening to and being with someone in depression and despair, is the test of real love. Docetism is the religious way to escape having love tested in the flesh. All of us are tempted to audit life rather than to participate fully and be tested by it. (p.38)

> Gnosticism, then and now, is characterised by claims to special knowledge held by an intellectual elite who are on their way to becoming super-spirits. (p.55)

> Sabellian believers, becoming like what they worship, will inevitably resort to being poseurs, persons who affect a particular manner or character as changing circumstances seem to require. This pervasive but pitiful compulsion in contemporary society to create for oneself an image or an identity is a symptom of a religious wasteland that has been given no confidence in a God-given identity. (p.76)

> Much of conventional Christianity today is Apollinarian. 'Don't ask questions, just have faith' ... Much of the appeal of cults has been, and still is, that they offer to turn our minds off (or over to a group or guru). Not ever having to use one's mind to think, to question, or to decide makes Apollinarian solutions perennially attractive. (p.108)

5.20 This reminds us that the Christian Church is always being challenged to conform to 'the way God has provided' and when we engage in mission as Christians, we need to point to that way and not be distracted from it. It is all too easy, however, for those who search for faith to be offered by us a less rigorous or a self-serving kind of Christianity. The fact that we ourselves often fall short in our Christian witness becomes clearer to us as we look back at the past tensions between heresy and orthodoxy. Yet we cannot forget the first sense in which we defined heresy and some, such as Robert van der Weyer, suggest we need to be heretics today in order to prevent the Church from stagnating into meaninglessness; heretical challenge forces the Church to account for itself.

The ontological proof

5.21 On the next stage of our journey, we must encounter those fathers of the Church who, in seeking to reach those who had not heard God's story, tried to show that belief in the Christian God was logical, aesthetically desirable and the only way of supporting a sense of coherence and harmony. For example, in the eleventh century, St Anselm of Canterbury proposed a thought-system which aimed to show that atheism is a logically indefensible position.[14] He said:

> Now, Lord, since it is you who gives understanding to faith, grant me to understand as well as you think fit, that you exist as we believe, and that you are what we believe you to be. We believe that you are that thing than which nothing greater can be thought.[15]

5.22 This argument can be formulated as follows:

> If the greatest being possible does not exist, then it is possible that there exists a being greater than the greatest being possible.
>
> It is not possible that there exists a being greater than the greatest being possible.
>
> Therefore:
>
> The greatest being possible exists.[16]

5.23 This argument produced objections immediately, but has remained an overriding philosophical debate ever since. Aquinas, Hume and Kant rejected it, while Descartes, Spinoza and Leibniz accepted it from their respective standpoints.

5.24 In the thirteenth century, St Thomas Aquinas (1224/5–74) produced his famous 'five ways' of showing that there must be God, even if God is an unknowable mystery. Consequently, each of his five ways begins with the effect of a divine act and is traced back to God as its cause. From the observation that things move, Aquinas discovers God as First Mover; similarly God is found to be First Cause in the chain of causation; God is found to be necessary of himself, the cause of all goodness and perfection, and finally the originator of teleology whereby all things tend towards a purposeful end.

5.25 In the history of ideas, much time and thought has been spent on the evaluation of the ontological proof, but as far as mission is concerned, we may say that the act of living and behaving as if (and only if) the gospel were true, constitutes a working out of the truth of what Christianity is. Indeed, some historians contend that Aquinas's *Summa contra Gentiles* is intended to be missionary, especially towards followers of a certain kind of Islam, as are the writings of other Church fathers such as Bernard of Clairvaux. This means that the continuing arguments over the logic of the ontological proof do not affect the importance of acting in mission. If this sounds a bit like Pascal's wager (it is better to believe in God than not believe, because if you die and there's nothing, you have lost nothing, but if you die and there is, you've lost everything), this is not intended. Rather, the fathers of the Church tried to show that belief in and proclamation of the Christian gospel enriches life to such an extent that no other epistemological position can offer exactly the same quality of life. Therefore, if we return to St Anselm:

> God of truth,
> I ask that I may receive,
> so that my joy may be full.
> Meanwhile, let my mind meditate on it,
> let my tongue speak of it,
> let my heart love it,
> let my mouth preach it,
> let my soul hunger for it,
> my flesh thirst for it,
> and my whole being desire it,
> until I enter into the joy of my Lord,
> who is God one and triune, blessed forever. Amen.[17]

The medieval worldview

5.26   We now have to consider the way in which people saw the world to be ordered in the medieval period, for the worldview at this time was ordered and hierarchical. The feudal system ensured that people understood that they were born into a particular station in life and related to others in their society according to a prescribed system. The earth formed the centre of their cosmology, with a fixed vault of stars wheeling above it. Beyond this was heaven, the abode of God. Imposed on this was a system of sense-making that placed religious thinking as the ultimate sense-maker. We may see an example of this in the Hereford *Mappa Mundi*, a map of the known world with Jerusalem placed firmly in the centre: the centre of the geographical space, the centre of God's activity, the centre of the human heart.

5.27   In this period, there was therefore a coherence between the physical life and the spiritual life; the two were superimposed in such a way as to make belief the rationale for the experience of being alive. Society and culture were infused by being Christian, even if, at the popular level, this was mediated by superstition and the nearness of death and suffering.[18] The role of fate, as operating absolutely in people's lives, was especially important in the worldview, where lives could be cut short at any time. Consequently, if we journey for a few moments with Chaucer's (*c.* 1340–1400) pilgrims, we will learn that:

> The destinee, ministre general,
> That executeth in the world over al
> The purveiaunce that god hath seyn biforn,
> So strong it is that, though the world hath sworn
> The contrarie of a thyng by ye or nay,
> Yet somtyme it shal fallen on a day
> That falleth nat eft withinne a thousand yeer.
> For certeinly, oure appetites heer,
> Be it of werre, or pees, or hate, or love,
> Al this is reuled by the sighte above ...
>
> What is this world? What asketh men to have?
> Now with his love, now in his colde grave
> Allone, withouten any compagnie[19]

Figure 7 The Hereford *Mappa Mundi*

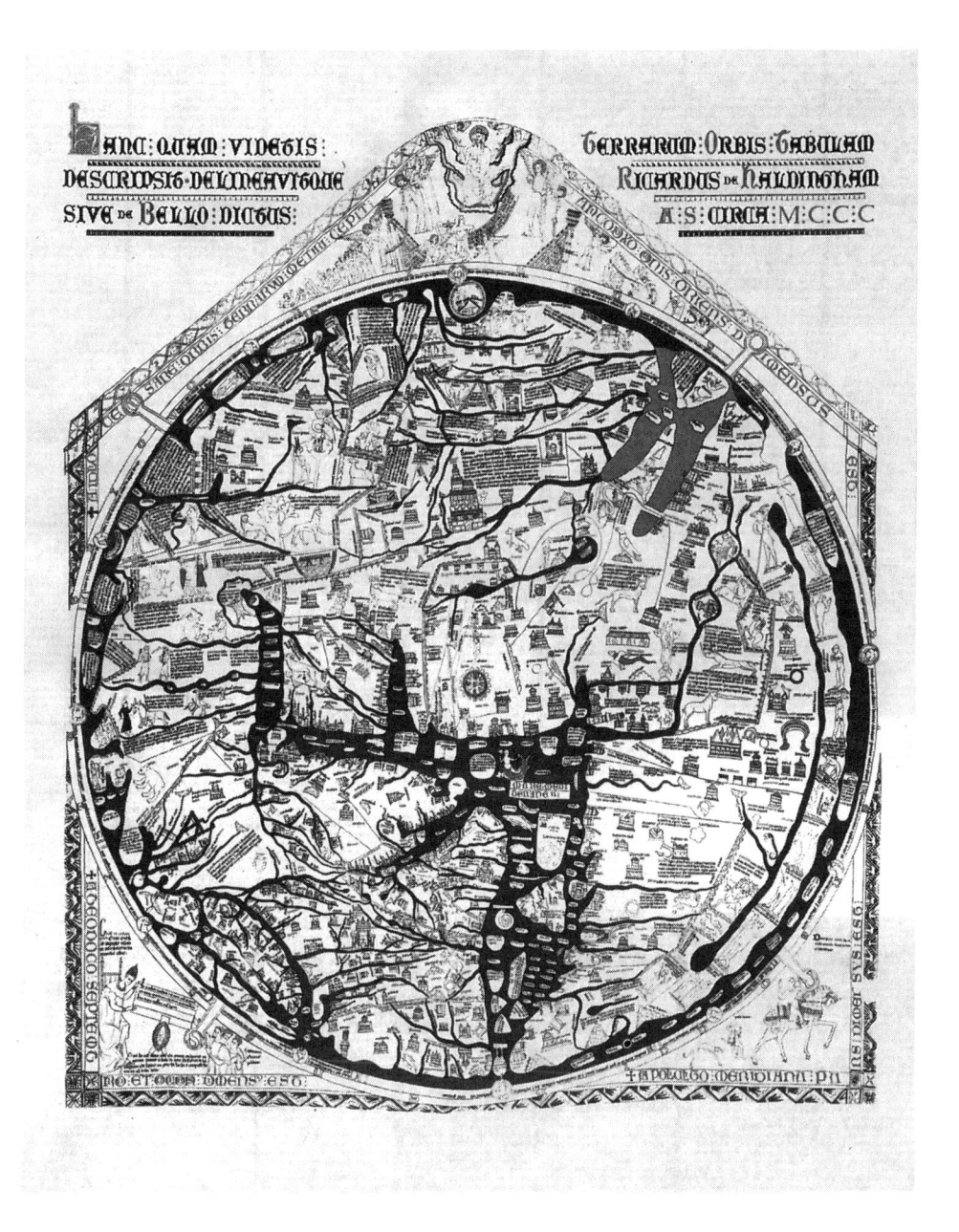

5.28 In such a worldview, the afterlife is particularly imbued with the richness of human imagining. Dante immediately springs to mind, with his vision at the end of the *Paradiso* of the arrangement of saints in the Rose and the sublime vision of the Trinity as two brilliant rainbows from which flame goes forth, an overwhelming insight into the 'Love that moves the Sun and th'other stars'.[20] Similarly, the fourteenth-century English poem *Pearl*, for example, turns the loss of a baby daughter into a glorious vision of heaven in which the daughter returns to the grieving parent to promise the unimaginable joy and beauty in the paradise beyond, for all God's promises are true. At the other extreme, the artist Hieronymus Bosch (born *c.* 1450) employed complex symbolic imaginings of the destruction and torture of the damned. These imaginative acts of looking forward were urgent and important, and the transcendental reality not just a matter of promise and hope, but a way of indicating the need for change in the present.

From Renaissance to Reformation

5.29 As feudal society began to break down, Renaissance thinking, influenced by the translation of Arab philosophy and science, began to challenge the medieval system of ideas. In particular, the cultivation of excellence in the arts and sciences and the pursuit of order and control ushered in an attitude of enquiry and refinement. This has also been seen as a switch from looking to the vault of heaven for inspiration and authority, to the lower world of animals, plants and objects for systems of understanding and sense-making, bringing with it a significant change in perception and thought. For some this meant engaging in a struggle between the unquestioned Christian framework of ordinary life and the spirit of questioning. The Christian paradigm was also necessarily the source of the Church's political power. It is not surprising, then, that the Church often reacted against what appeared to be the discovery of new and dangerous knowledge. Leonardo da Vinci's notebooks, for example, suggest the range of Renaissance enquiry, for he meditates on science and knowledge, the universe, the powers of nature, flight, the arts, architecture and reflections on life itself.

5.30 Among his fables, or parables, Leonardo (1452–1519) returns several times to the image of a moth or butterfly around a candle:

> The vain and wandering moth, not content with its power to fly through the air at its ease, and overcome by the seductive flame of the candle, decided to fly into it; but its joyous movement was the cause of instant woe; for in the flame its delicate wings were consumed. And the hapless moth dropped all burnt at the foot of the candlestick. After much lamentation and repentance it wiped the tears from its streaming eyes and raising its face exclaimed: 'O False light! how many like me must thou have miserably deceived in times past; and if my desire was to see light ought I not to have distinguished the sun from the false glimmer of dirty tallow?'[21]

5.31 In a further fable, the light replies 'Thus do I treat whoever does not know how to use me aright' and Leonardo comments 'This applies to those who, when they see before them carnal and worldly delight, hasten to them like the butterfly, without ever taking thought as to their nature, which they will learn to know to their shame and loss.'[22]

5.32 Leonardo identifies the descent into 'necromancy' and superstitious practices in the Church and makes important distinctions between the living faith and the 'dead' nature of Church culture and in his 'prophecies' remarks on abuses in the practice of the faith, particularly involving money transactions. In this way he prefigures the disturbance and unrest that led to the Reformation. The true light is in danger of being eclipsed by followers of other lesser lights. Human beings in this culture are seduced by the trivial and by worldly pleasures and this is the hallmark of such a society.

5.33 Erasmus (c. 1469–1536) understood this, which is why he wrote his book *In Praise of Folly* in the way he did. In the letter to Martin Dorp, he writes:

> The truth of the gospel slips more pleasantly into the mind and takes firmer grip there if it is attractively clothed than it would if it were presented undisguised ... I saw how ordinary men were corrupted by opinions of the most foolish kind in every walk of life. I longed to find a remedy more than I hope for success. And I believed I had found a means whereby I could somehow insinuate myself into these over-indulged souls and cure them by giving them pleasure.[23]

The Search for Faith

5.34   Here, then, we can see that critical ideas were introduced into public circulation to expose the disparity between what was seen as the core of faith carried in mission by the Christian Church and the distortions of that faith brought about by the culture and by the problems in the Church. This observed disparity then led to new theological thinking arising from a dialectic with the criticism. In this case abuses relating to God's saving promises led to theological concentration on the nature of salvation.[24] Protestantism was then erected on a number of issues, two of which included: a reaction against the political and power structures of the Church, and the theological distortions arising from misuse of that power, for example, the idea that money could buy heavenly life. At the same time, criticism of abuses led to important reaction within the Catholic paradigm; for example, Ignatius Loyola and the Society of Jesus brought a fresh missionary emphasis to the faith.

5.35   Martin Luther (1483–1546), himself branded a 'heretic', formulated the idea of justification by grace through faith by a return to the biblical heart of teaching about salvation – a foundational re-reading of Pauline teaching. David Bosch has identified five key features of the new Protestant paradigm: justification by faith; the inherent evil of the world; the subjective dimension of salvation; the priesthood of all believers and the centrality of the Scriptures. John Calvin (1509–64) looked to establishment of a theocracy on earth by a process of radical transformation through the Spirit. These outworkings of new theology meant that in western Europe the Church offered simultaneously a number of diverse ways to be Christian.

5.36   This diversity has also had profound implications for mission, for the mission of the Church to reflect God's reconciling will for the whole creation became from this period also the history of reconciliation between parts of the Christian Church. Mission includes a move towards unity, and towards those acts of reconciliation between churches which are reflected in worship, witness and service and which illustrate God's intention for the world and for all human beings. The dialogues and agreements which are hallmarks of the twentieth century, such as the ARCIC discussions between Anglicans and Roman Catholic churches, Methodist–Anglican dialogue, the Meissen agreement between the Church of England and the German Lutheran churches, the Porvoo agreement between the Church of England and the Scandinavian and Baltic churches and the overtures between the Roman Catholic Church and the Orthodox, and between Roman Catholics and Lutherans, demonstrate to western society an impulse towards dialogue and reconsideration in a world of fragmentation and lost direction. Moreover, such dialogues illustrate a simple and basic truth: that Christians are impelled to talk about God and their understanding of what God has done.

5.37 One of the profound effects of the fragmentation of the Christian Church on the history of ideas and values in the west was the rise of philosophical scepticism or doubt.[25] In the face of competing Christian truth systems, different political entities and increasing discovery about the world, a culture of doubt began to arise that valued sceptical testing of ideas over inherited faith. The search for coherence between the physical and spiritual realms therefore often became relegated in some places to the arcane or the mystical, as in this poem of Henry Vaughan (1621–95), where he speaks of coming to know God as a mysterious experience of the night:

> Through that pure Virgin shrine,
> That sacred veil drawn o'er thy glorious noon
> That men might look and live as glow-worms shine,
> And face the moon:
> Wise Nicodemus saw such light
> As made him know his God by night.
>
> Most blest believer he!
> Who in that land of darkness and blind eyes
> Thy long expected healing wings could see,
> When thou didst rise,
> And what can never more be done,
> Did at mid-night speak with the Sun! ...
>
> There is in God (some say)
> A deep, but dazzling darkness; as men here
> Say it is late and dusky, because they
> See not all clear;
> O for that night! where I in him
> Might live invisible and dim.[26]

The Enlightenment

5.38 We have passed through the various tunnels of fragmentation, viewed a maze of passages and now enter the Enlightenment. Here, we may see that a profound shift in the history of ideas came about during the period known as the Enlightenment. Indeed, there is a significant movement in the twentieth century to blame the Enlightenment for the mental framework that makes it so difficult for many people to believe the truth of the Christian Gospel. The chief proponent of this criticism is Bishop Lesslie Newbigin whose books on the subject of gospel and culture[27] have had much influence and given rise to a contemporary theological movement.

5.39 The philosophers of the Enlightenment period are distinguished by their various forms of enquiry into how we know anything at all. How do human beings acquire knowledge? What is the nature of understanding? What was being put to the test here was the nature and quality of human reason: was it reasonable, or rational to believe in God? Scholasticism was for the most part, though not entirely, disdained. Another point made by David Bosch is that these philosophers disposed their thought in logical forms much more akin to mathematical thought than to traditional discourse (see the version of Anselm's proof above) and that this inevitably moved away from the thought forms and expressions which were traditionally employed to speak about God.

5.40 In his *Discourse on Method*, René Descartes (1596–1650) took his readers on a journey to understanding. In this work, he reminds us that our minds must be considered finite while God is incomprehensible and infinite. He then provides us with meditations on: why we can doubt all things; the non-existence of what is doubted; God as the cause of ideas; the nature of truth and falsity; and the proof of God and understanding from imagination. Baruch Spinoza (1632–77), however, suggested that in order to achieve salvation we must free ourselves from emotions and use reason to obtain an intellectual love of God. Gottfried Leibniz (1646–1716) was much engaged in an argument for moderation of the sceptical view in his *Discourse on Metaphysics*, while John Locke (1632–1704) introduced 'the idea' as fundamental, examining epistemology itself. Bishop George Berkeley (1685–1753) took this further, moving from ideas to 'idealism'. God's continuing perception keeps things in existence and the things themselves are to be thought of as collections of ideas. The strongest opponent of all rational arguments concerning God emerged in the figure of David Hume (1711–76) who saw all religious debates as futile and sought to demonstrate the failure of arguments about God. Immanuel Kant (1724–1804) wrote in response to Hume, most famously in the *Critique of Pure Reason*, but ultimately agreeing with him that we cannot ourselves have knowledge of ultimate reality.

5.41 The Enlightenment, then, is the result of much philosophical dialogue involving argument and response, feeling as much for effective method in philosophical discourse as it is dealing with the theological arguments.

5.42 Newbigin's principal indictment of the Enlightenment thinking is not so much what was actually written (to which he acknowledges debt), but the effect it had on western culture through the history of ideas. In particular he feels that the Enlightenment created categories of public truth and private opinion, and that religious belief became relegated to the latter category. For this reason, Newbigin has written extensively on the need of the Church today to re-enter the realm of 'public truth'. Thus:

> Christian faith became – for most people – a private and domestic matter strictly separated from the public worlds of politics and economics. The Bible no longer provided the framework within which world history was understood. World history was now taught as the history of civilization with – quite naturally – the civilization of western Europe as its climax. The other way of understanding history, which found its climax in the person of a first century Jew, was relegated to a separate department of 'religious instruction' and treated as a parable of the history of the human soul.[28]

5.43 For Newbigin, then, the coherent world of the *Mappa Mundi* has been skewed so that the human map has replaced that of God. The spiritual map has been interiorised and marginalised. Consequently, Newbigin sees the notion of the transcendent as particularly diminished. However, Newbigin does not consider the possible advantages of taking religious discourse out of the political wrangling in the public arena. Further, he does not allow for the embedding of the Christian narrative in language and culture such that foundational shapes of Christian witness continue to underlie the behaviour, endeavour and invention of western society. The reaction of Newbigin and his movement to this split between public and private discourse is a call to rediscover the gospel as public truth. While it sounds as though this must be an essential part of Christian witness, we have to remember that there is a distinction between theocracy and public truth. An added difficulty here is Newbigin's apparent disregard of today's religious plurality, and the contribution made to our society by those of other faith traditions, since instituting the gospel as public truth *could* mean a refusal of tolerance and dialogue. It is perhaps preferable to argue that no human order is perfect, but mission theology looks towards a kingdom in which God's order prevails. The gospel becomes effective as public truth when Christians become involved in public issues informed by their faith.

5.44 If now we board a train for faster progress through the Industrial Revolution, we can see out of the window that the increasing role of automated processes created pressure to understand the place of human beings in the world and in the universe, biologically, socially, and economically. For example, the development and exploitation of the pump provided a context for understanding the action of the human heart. The Industrial Revolution also particularly highlighted the question of class, considered hierarchically and as holding different types of power. Ideological systems such as Marxism could also arise by making economics the dominant perspective for making recommendations about how human beings should live and conduct themselves. Similarly, with the rise of Darwinism, these conclusions about the world and its processes had to be tested against the deeply embedded view of the Creator God and the sense of being 'other' than the animal world.

5.45 These changes, which emphasised the status and role of (mostly male) human beings trapped in time, created the conditions for Friedrich Nietzsche (1844–1900) to suggest: 'Modern men, obtuse to all Christian nomenclature, no longer feel the gruesome superlative that struck a classical taste in the paradoxical formula "god on the cross"'[29] and 'it seems to me that the religious instinct is indeed in the process of growing powerfully – but the theistic satisfaction it refuses with deep suspicion.'[30] He proposed a system 'beyond good and evil', a system in which God's operation in the world need not be debated at all. Human beings are made in the image of their higher humanity or super-self: the one who overcomes without any reference to outside or transcendental agency. This is not a pessimistic vision of a world without God, but an affirmatory vision of the best that we can be. Such a viewpoint also provides us with a reference point for the school of theology known as Sea of Faith (see Chapter 4) which sees God not as supernatural agency, but as the summation of human ideals. According to this view, God is just a word which can be applied to the best that we are or can become.[31] Speculation about a supernatural destiny is futile. Discussion about the last things is not necessary to these thought systems and it is therefore not surprising that theologians within the Church have recently shown new interest in recovering the eschatological dimension. For mission, this is certainly crucial, otherwise mission theology would be reduced to describing a biblical utopia, the only rationale for the existence of which would be its inclusiveness and stability.

Language and silence

5.46   As we move in our journey ever faster into the twentieth century, we discover, with Einstein, that what we observe depends on whether we are on the train or standing on the station. The demonstration that there are no privileged reference frames in the physical world, might then make us think harder about taking ideas for granted. Relativity may have no direct relationship to relativism, but we may have to revise our preconceptions about ideas when we recall that Nietzsche (who was a philologist) tells us that language can be considered a system of untruths, because words only approximate to reality. He says:

> What therefore is truth? A mobile army of metaphors, metonymies, anthropomorphisms: in short a sum of human relations which become poetically and rhetorically intensified, metamorphosed, adorned, and after long usage seems to a nation fixed, canonic, and binding; truths are illusions of which one has forgotten that they are illusions; worn-out metaphors which have become powerless to affect the sense; coins which have their obverse effaced and now are no longer of account but merely as metal.[32]

5.47   In this way, Nietzsche describes the scenario for one of the defining debates in the twentieth-century history of ideas. In the twentieth century, language and meaning come increasingly under scrutiny, so the question is not 'What are the limits of human understanding?' but 'What are the limits of language and of semantic reference frames?'. Freudianism, for example, generated a new set of ideas when it was suggested that people can use mental symbols which when reported concealed the truth. Talking to an interpreter, the 'real' meanings (whether theirs or the interpreter's) could be liberated from the subconscious mind.[33] Sigmund Freud (1856–1939) also pointed up the role of memory and forgetting in human suffering, and pointed to the presence of intense mental pain. The dream world could be seen as an alternative place for working out problems and difficulties as well as suppressed desires. The transcendental world was locked up in the head.

5.48   Carl Gustav Jung (1875–1961), breaking away from Freud, then sought to show that the 'collective unconscious' could be considered the encyclopaedic memory for all symbolic structures including religious symbolism. Further, getting away from God, and finding ways to get rid of guilt could be a liberating and self-affirming experience.[34] It is notable that Jungian analysis and some forms of psychotherapy based on Jungian ideas are popular with those whose search for faith requires a strong emphasis on self-discovery.

5.49   Where language is slippery and the richness of religious discourse devalued, we can see how the question of the place and role of signs and symbols might be seen to be absorbed in the dream world or the unconscious. We can also see that the influence of this thinking makes the role of silence more acute. In T. S. Eliot's *The Waste Land*, dreamlike snatches of voices carry the suggestions of Christian stories: there is a hint of Gethsemane, a distorted glimpse of the Damascus road experience. Death, dying and loss of articulation characterise the 'Unreal City'. Twentieth-century living and loss of personal loving relationship become tangled to suggest sterility and little hope of salvation. Here, Eliot asks the question that still preoccupies us: what coherent, underlying structure can possibly make sense of all this?

5.50   Similarly, if we continue our journey across the wastelands of two world wars and, in particular, the events of the Holocaust, we can see how acts of inhumanity and genocide around the world have led some religious thinkers to suggest that there is no longer a function for a theology of hope. If there is no theological understanding which can make sense of the atrocities of the Holocaust then we should be content to say nothing.[35] To continue to witness to a loving God who intends good for his people is a mockery and an arrogance. Faced with this charge, we may find it difficult to respond, unless we remember what Elie Wiesel says in *Night*, when the despairing cry 'Where is God now?' at the hanging of a boy, is met by the reply 'He is hanging here on this gallows.'[36]

5.51 Ludwig Wittgenstein (1889–1951) also gives us important clues about the range and limits of meanings in relation to language. Thus the way in which we witness or proclaim may be subject to the mendacity to which Nietzsche pointed and Wittgenstein elucidates. We are not capable of saying what we mean, only of showing by example. The distinction between showing and saying is an important contribution. George Steiner says:

> The greatest of modern philosophers was also the one most profoundly intent on escaping from the spiral of language. Wittgenstein's entire work starts out by asking whether there is any verifiable relation between the word and the fact. That which we call fact may well be a veil spun by language to shroud the mind from reality. Wittgenstein compels us to wonder whether reality can be spoken of, when speech is merely a kind of infinite regression, words being spoken of other words. Wittgenstein pursued this dilemma with passionate austerity. The famous closing proposition of the Tractatus [whereof we cannot speak, thereof we must be silent] is not a claim for the potentiality of philosophic statement such as Descartes advanced. On the contrary; it is a drastic retreat from the confident authority of traditional metaphysics. It leads to the equally famous conclusion: 'It is clear that Ethics cannot be expressed'. Wittgenstein would include in the class of inexpressible (what he calls the mystical) most of the traditional areas of philosophic speculation. Language can only deal meaningfully with a special, restricted segment of reality. The rest, and it is presumably the much larger part, is silence.[37]

5.52 In such culture, filled with the memory of the dead, it is unsurprising that fragmentation of a severe kind should occur. Further, it is also not surprising that groups have emerged which indict Christianity for not being descriptive of their cause. Some women, for example, redefining themselves

The Search for Faith

in terms of feminist theory, find themselves obliged to reject Christianity as having nothing to offer them, being both hierarchical and patriarchal. Some theologians, such as Daphne Hampson, have argued themselves to be 'post-Christian', having gone beyond the confines of a religious system which contributes to the marginalisation of women.

> The yew tree points up. It has a Gothic shape.
>
> The eyes lift after it and find the moon.
>
> The moon is my mother. She is not sweet like Mary.
>
> Her blue garments unloose small bats and owls.
>
> How I would like to believe in tenderness –
>
> The face of the effigy, gentled by candles,
>
> Bending, on me in particular, its mild eyes.
>
> I have fallen a long way. Clouds are flowering
>
> Blue and mystical over the face of the stars.
>
> Inside the church, the saints will all be blue,
>
> Floating on their delicate feet over the cold pews,
>
> Their hands and faces stiff with holiness.
>
> The moon sees nothing of this. She is bald and wild.
>
> And the message of the yew tree is blackness – blackness and silence.[38]

5.53 Sylvia Plath is excluded from the church, relegated to the graveyard with her familiars the moon, the bats, the owls. Despite the despairing desire for the image of womanhood the church offers, she cannot accept it. What is left to her is the void of darkness and silence. In the realm of historic Christianity, she has no contribution to make. It is suggested in response that such women are misconstruing Christianity because of their own constriction by a theoretical position which is inconsistent with the experience of faith. For example, the vulnerability of Christ on the cross is seen as refuting the claim that Christianity is patriarchal and dominating. Only the historic traditions of Christianity are so dominating and need, through women's critique, to repent. A new kind of Christianity is open to women who bring their insights to bear. Theologians such as Grace Jantzen, Rosemary Radford Reuther, Janet Martin Soskice, Elisabeth Schussler Fiorenza and Mary Grey, are all contributing ideas to the Church about its witness and proclamation by and for women.

5.54 Other people searching for faith will argue that the Church has nothing to say about sexuality or the experience of being creatures and that this merely leads to repressiveness based on gender or sexual orientation.[39] Again, these are areas in which there may seem to be an ominous silence, and the witness of the Church may appear defective where it does not address these issues comprehensively.

5.55 For example, the poet W. B. Yeats disagreed with Christianity because he believed it was constructed on two negative ideas: the virgin womb and empty tomb.[40] Yeats wanted physicality, sexuality and corporeality to affirm the world against death and silence. This also links with the criticisms made by feminist theologians. Ursula King writes:

> Feminist spirituality lays greater emphasis on immanence and correlations than on separateness. It also stresses concrete embodiment and advocates an embodied rather than an idealized, abstract spirituality divorced from everyday experience. Thus many women reclaim the power of the erotic as a feature and source of spiritual energy.[41]

5.56 Further, in considering the position of those who feel marginalised and cut off from (or by) mainstream Christianity, we cannot overlook the existentialist rejection which sees the extension of silence to include suicide. Texts such as Kafka's *The Trial* and Sartre's *Nausea* are brilliant and terrifying expositions of how the world becomes distorted and unliveable without adequate reference frames. However, the choice for suicide may also emerge out of happiness or a feeling of completeness, like Keats's 'now more than ever seems it rich to die'. This is illustrated by an example:

Scott (not his real name) was a young man in his early twenties. He had served his time at a trade and had a good job. His bosses were happy with his work and he got on well with his friends. His parents were separated but he got on well with both. He was good friends with his brother and his brother's fiancée and he was a part of a group of young people who went about

The Search for Faith

together. He had a car, interests, holidays. There were no difficulties or problems. One weekend he drove to one of his favourite parts of the countryside and took his own life. The goodbye note expressed his love for his family. This was his choice. Trying to respect this choice helped his mother a little as she grappled with coming to terms with losing her son.

5.57 In the Inspector Morse episode called *Cherubim and Seraphim*, Inspector Morse looks for misery and pain in the lives of teenagers who committed suicide. In fact, he cannot solve the case until he realises that the suicides are caused by a drug and disco culture which confers feelings of ecstasy and having achieved the ultimate. The frustration and bewilderment of Inspector Morse as he tries to understand a youth culture based on joy are a reminder also to Christians that the culture into which we speak the truth of God's promises may assimilate this truth but its re-expression may be quite novel.

5.58 Existentialist thinking from Heidegger onwards attempts to rescue the world of thought from encroaching silence by looking to the recovery of the transcendental dimension.

> Two forms move among the dead, high sleep
>
> Who by his highness quiets them, high peace
>
> Upon whose shoulders even the heavens rest,
>
> Two brothers. And a third form, she that says
>
> Good-by in the darkness, speaking quietly there,
>
> To those who cannot say good-by themselves.[42]

5.59 The 'flash of voice' that maintains our ability to speak of what lies beyond death; the presence of an articulate wisdom, is apposite. Consequently, in such a thought system, the theology of Christ as *Logos*, the Word becomes an important concept for seeing how death and silence can be overcome by the presence of the *Logos* in those places which seem abandoned by God.

5.60 We must also deal with the critique advanced by, for example, Iris Murdoch under the general idea that there is no God but Good. In today's society, the principle of Good must be recovered, but its attachment to a deity who sets the standard for goodness is not only unnecessary but anachronistic. This is not to say that the history of religious moral philosophy as it derives from Christianity is to be rejected, but it becomes the background colouring for principles in which human beings are the main and only players:

> Christianity now, faced with the withdrawal of belief from the supernatural, may be tempted by various forms of 'cosmic answer' of which Jung's view is one. Religion as a sort of science. I attach, as I have been arguing, great importance to the concept of a transcendent good as an idea (properly interpreted) to both morality and religion ... We need a theology which can continue without God. Why not call such a reflection a form of moral philosophy? All right, so long as it treats of those matters of 'ultimate concern', our experience of the unconditioned and our continued sense of what is holy.[43]

5.61 To return to the post-modern world, we may have to consider very carefully the Ven. David Atkinson's description of our times as the *Ashtray of Modernity*. Here, the 'butt ends of our days and ways' as T. S. Eliot put it, are stubbed out in the crucible of ideas and we run vainly to and fro trying to relight this one and then that one for a short while. For some, our pick'n'mix culture is really a sifting of ashes:

> So the past becomes a theme park, for the amusement of the visiting tourist. For instance, Gregorian plainsong (popular for chilling out to after taking the drug Ecstasy, it is said) is now highly commercial. Record shops have shelves of it. But the truth about plainsong, that it is an ancient expression of collective prayer, is largely missed. This is one more illustration of the opacity of religion in a post-modernist culture. It is that very opacity that has rendered religious style and experiences now safe to play with – there is no danger of their underlying meaning taking hold.
>
> Experience is the touchstone of post-modernism, but only good experience. If religious movements succumb to post-modernism, they must do so by suppressing the difficult and painful bits of their message. Worship must 'feel good' and offer a 'spiritual high' ...

Belief in the real experience of a real God is definitely not a post-modernist position; it is far too uncomfortable and disturbing, post-modernism chooses the bits it likes and discards the rest.[44]

5.62 For others, the search for meaning is a positive and strengthening experience, in which the ashes hold many possibilities for rekindling. Those who search for faith may be precisely those who fall into this category and it is up to us to provide them with the Christian witness as the source of a light which never dies.

5.63 Now we have to look back at our journey through the history of ideas. We have only stopped briefly at some of the many stations, not gone out to explore the town thoroughly. Yet each of these stopping places presents a challenge to the historic witness of the Christian faith and some, as we have seen, have offered branch lines to distort the continuity of that witness. Other passengers have got on whose ideas have affected the dialogue with the carriers of Christianity and have added new perspectives to their imagining of the final destination.

5.64 But perhaps in our time the Good News can go no further, because it is no longer clear which are termini and which is the continuation of the line. We have perhaps two options; the first is that we can get out for a while and explore where the line goes – which we have done in our various chapters – or trust in the recapitulation of history: 'it is easy to miss Him at the turn of a civilisation'.[45] We may trust that a time will come when human beings will seek again for coherence out of fragmentation, a new story of restoration in which the Christian epistemological framework will again offer its vision of reconciliation and hope. In that case, we need no longer sit on the rails, but fly away. But we may also properly argue that it is part of the missionary task not to fly off the rails but to endure in solidarity with others.

5.65 Until the world returns to God, then, we have Newbigin's argument in his book *Proper Confidence*:

> Through most of human history, religion has been the most powerful factor in the shaping of culture. To look outside of the gospel for a starting point for the demonstration of the reasonableness of the gospel is itself a contradiction of the gospel, for it implies that we look for the logos elsewhere than in Jesus ...

Until then, my commitment to the truth of the gospel is a commitment of faith. If I am further pressed to justify this commitment (as I have often been) my only response has to be a personal confession. The story is not my construction. In ways that I cannot fully understand but always through the witness of those who went before me in the company of those called to be witnesses, I have been laid hold of and charged with the responsibility of telling this story.[46]

5.66 This represents a back-to-the-wall approach to our culture, in which the residue of the global character of the Christian message experience becomes concentrated into the self as witness and testimony. Learning and change are resisted, for Newbigin is a Christian who can be tested and not found wanting. The strength of the story in him must attract others; a giving away of the gift into the dark world of contemporary culture cannot be risked.

5.67 Though we may admire this steadfastness and powerful adherence to the task of witness, what Newbigin says may undermine the missionary quest. In this chapter we have seen that the Christian faith can and does take risks and that any one contemporary situation may look very different when viewed from the perspective of history. The Church, then, does enter into dialogue with the world in the expectation that God is at work there and must seek to share its message of hope to those whose mental framework has been shaped by the inheritance of thought systems which have become the *Zeitgeist* of our world today. By bringing our Christian faith and the language of our salvation into places of doubt, transformation can take place. For it was only through a culture that could find significance in a dead sheep that we are able to experience the richness of the symbolism that imbues the Lamb of God, discovered at the throne of glory at the end of all that is.

Summary

KEY WORDS

- post-modern - orthodoxy - heresy - Trinity - ontological proof - five ways - Protestantism - dialogues - scepticism - Enlightenment - public truth - feminist theology

A look at the characteristics of the post-modern world might suggest to some people that we live in a totally godless society. If generations go by who know little about Christianity or any other religious tradition, or who have heard religion reduced merely to babble, then surely the missionary task of the Church is severely threatened and perhaps cannot be sustained?

In order to respond to this, it is necessary to formulate an historical overview of the development of Christian thinking in the context of the history of ideas. We need to find out how we have arrived at this kind of culture and what of the inherited tradition remains for us to work with. In particular, it is necessary to examine three trends in the history of ideas which have consequences for how we think about things today. These are: the effect of 'heretical' teaching on Christian belief; the emphasis on human reason during the Enlightenment; the threat of death and silence in the twentieth century.

The development of Christian theology, setting out what we understand about God and the way God works, has been a gradual process which derives much of its cutting edge from challenges to its primary teaching from other Christian thinkers. The response to 'heretical' views produced more clarity on the notion of Jesus as fully human and fully divine and helped to shape the theology of the Trinity. Side-effects of heretical thinking, particularly those which shape theology for our own ends, work against the clarification of what we believe and can still litter our thinking about God today.

Some Christian thinkers can be shown to have made thinking itself into a missionary act. Thus, the various arguments for God, such as the ontological proof, have been designed to show that atheism is a logically indefensible position. However, such arguments also depended on the prevailing worldview. Where the human and divine worlds mapped on to one another, such arguments made good sense; when invention and discovery in the history of progress began to place more emphasis on the human world, new thinking began to challenge the role of Christian orthodoxy. Where Christian practice fell short of Christian ideals, this too caused a culture of questioning, requiring response and redress by the Church.

During the period known as the Enlightenment, philosophers began to ponder the limits of human knowledge and to discuss the efficacy of human reason. One of the important effects of this was to bring about a separation between public and private roles for thought, such that religious belief became seen to belong to the private sphere of a person's life. The liberation of Christian thinking from the private realm back into the public arena has been seen as a crucial task for the mission of the Church in the present age, a view which is particularly propounded by Bishop Lesslie Newbigin. Further, other ideological positions arising from the history of progress can be seen to have further eroded the place of Christian thought even in the private sphere. This has led to philosophical thought-systems in which the supremacy of the human person, *qua* human, has left no room or necessity for God.

In the twentieth century there has been fresh emphasis on the limits of human thought, especially in terms of how we express ourselves. The experience of two world wars and the fragmentation of societies has asked whether our language is adequate to deal with the totality of our experience and whether or not our ability to discourse with each other is threatened by the inexpressible and by silence. Some people feel that Christianity itself is silent in respect of their own situation and challenge the Church to provide inclusive thinking which brings them fully into the promises of the Christian story.

The challenge, then, is to create a Christian apologetic which can speak effectively to the post-modern situation, and which is sensitive to the way in which we have inherited ideas. We cannot assume that people will be receptive to Christian ideas if the rest of their mental life is conditioned by the post-modern world, and we need to find images and ideas which can carry the meaningfulness of the Christian story back into people's lives.

Further reading

Allison, C. FitzSimons, *The Cruelty of Heresy*, Morehouse Publishing, 1994.

Bosch, David, *Transforming Mission*, Orbis, 1991.

General Synod Board of Education, *Tomorrow is Another Country: Education in a Post-modern World*, CHP, 1996.

Greenwood, Robin, *Transforming Priesthood*, SPCK, 1994.

Newbigin, Lesslie, *The Gospel in a Pluralist Society*, SPCK, 1989.

Things to do

- **AIM:** to think about our own faith in the context of living in today's world.
- **PURPOSE:** to see that telling the gospel story faithfully has a value for mission even if life makes that difficult.

BIBLE VERSE

> While he was making this defence, Festus exclaimed, 'You are out of your mind, Paul! Too much learning is driving you insane!' But Paul said, 'I am not out of my mind, most excellent Festus, but I am speaking the sober truth.' (Acts 26.24,25)

Things to do include:
a. Looking at pictures
b. Looking at videos
c. Explanations of faith
d. Discussion questions

1. PICTURES

Look at the post-modern image (see Figure 8).

Ask people to discuss with their neighbour what it says to them.

Figure 8 Tomorrow is another country

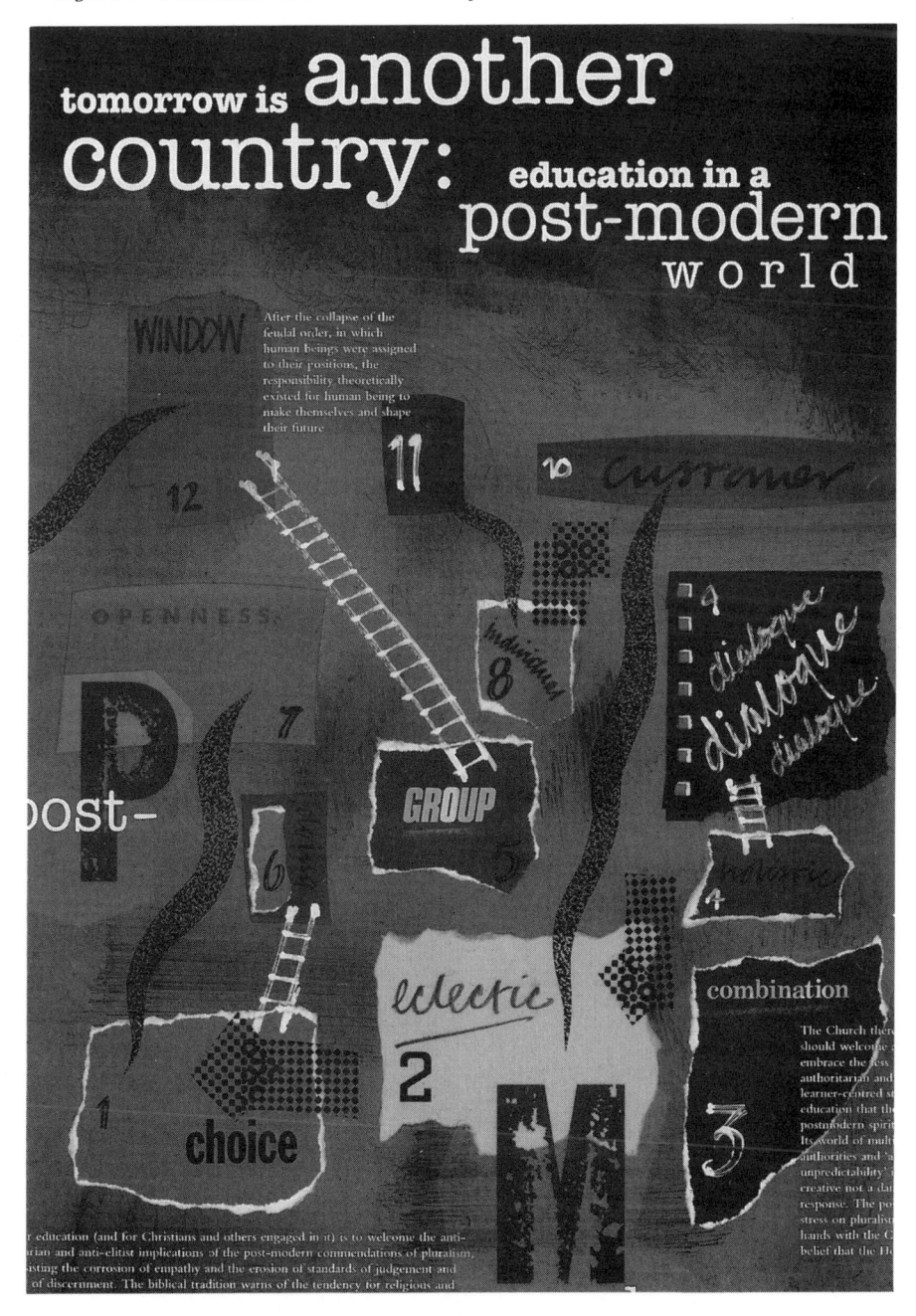

2. VIDEOS

Look at excerpts from some modern pop videos or video some advertisements (particularly those for cars). What is the 'story' in these videos?

3. FAITH SHARING

In small groups, ask one volunteer either to 'explain' his or her faith, or to give a testimony. Ask the listeners to say what impresses them about what is said. See if people feel there is a difference between 'rational explanation' and 'telling the story'.

As a group, consider whether it would be as easy or comfortable to share the same story at work, at a party, in another group or church. If people have done this, ask them to say what happened.

4. QUESTIONS FOR DISCUSSION

Choose some questions relevant to your group:

a. Does the world we live in seem hopeful or hopeless to you? How do other people you know think about it?

b. Do you think it is easier today to be an atheist than an agnostic?

c. Why do you think some people *cannot* believe the Christian Gospel?

d. Is reason as important as faith?

e. Is it more difficult to be a Christian in today's world?

f. Is it harder to make choices about what to believe?

Notes

1. · David Jones, 'A,a,a, Domine Deus', in *The Sleeping Lord and other Fragments*, Faber, 1974, p.9.
2. 'A Hard Beauty', Philip Sampson talks to Peter Greenaway, *Third Way*, December 1995, pp.12–15.
3. *Tomorrow is Another Country: Education in a Post-modern World*, CHP, 1996, p.9.

4. Duckworth, 1985.
5. For an excellent study of the way the idea of mission has changed through various historical 'paradigms', the reader is directed to David Bosch, *Transforming Mission*, Orbis, 1991.
6. See, for example, Leonardo Boff, *Trinity and Society*, Burns and Oates, 1988.
7. C. FitzSimons Allison, *The Cruelty of Heresy*, Morehouse Publishing, 1994, p.17.
8. Ibid., p.163.
9. For a fuller discussion of the development of Trinitarian theology, particularly as it relates to the requirements of today, see Robin Greenwood, *Transforming Priesthood*, SPCK, 1994, chapter 4.
10. *The Cruelty of Heresy*, op. cit., p.65.
11. See Lukas Vischer (ed.), *Spirit of God – Spirit of Christ: Ecumenical Reflections on the Filioque Controversy*, Faith and Order Paper no. 103, SPCK/WCC, 1981.
12. 'In the interests of gaining an understanding of the historical development of Christian theology, it seems to me vital that we do not attribute to earlier generations of Christians views which today seem to us to make good sense, but which were in fact explicitly anathema to them.' Letter to the *Church Times*, 26 January 1996. He refers here to contemporary notions that God suffers with us and that all will ultimately be saved.
13. *The Cruelty of Heresy*, op. cit.
14. *Proslogion*, chapters 2 and 3.
15. *Proslogion*, chapter 2 in *The Prayers and Meditations of St Anselm*, Penguin edition, 1973, p.244.
16. For clarity the version of Anselm's argument given in James W. Cornman, Keith Lehrer and George S. Pappas, *Philosophical Problems and Arguments: An Introduction*, Hackett Publishing Company, 1987, p.243 is used here.
17. *Proslogion*, chapter 26 in *The Prayers and Meditations of St Anselm*, op. cit., pp.266–7.
18. See especially Keith Thomas, *Religion and the Decline of Magic: Studies in Popular Beliefs in Sixteenth and Seventeenth Century England*, Peregrine edition, 1978, chapter 1.
19. Geoffrey Chaucer, 'The Knight's Tale' from *The Canterbury Tales*, ed. F. N. Robinson, OUP, 1957, pp. 33, 44.
20. Dante Alighieri, *The Divine Comedy*, Blackwell, 1981, p.769.
21. *The Notebooks of Leonardo da Vinci*, selected and edited by Irma A. Richter, OUP, 1980, p.239.
22. Ibid., pp.243–4.
23. Erasmus, *In Praise of Folly*, Penguin edition, 1971, p.216.
24. See *The Mystery of Salvation: The Story of God's Gift*, by the Doctrine Commission of the Church of England, CHP, 1996.
25. Cf. the use by liberation theologians of the phrase 'hermeneutics of suspicion'.
26. 'The Night', in Alan Rudrum (ed.), *Complete Poems of Henry Vaughan*, Penguin edition, 1976, pp.289–90.

27. For example, *The Other Side of 1984*, WCC, 1984; *The Gospel in a Pluralist Society*, SPCK, 1989.
28. Lesslie Newbigin, *The Other Side of 1984: Questions for the Churches*, WCC, 1984, p.22.
29. Friedrich Nietzsche, *Beyond Good and Evil*, trans. Walter Kaufmann, Vintage edition, 1966, p.60.
30. Ibid., p.66.
31. See the Revd Anthony Freeman, *God in Us*, SCM, 1993 and also the writings of Don Cupitt.
32. 'Truth and falsity in an ultra-moral sense' (*Über Wahrheit und Luge im außermoralischen Sinn*) in *Truth and Illusion: The Philosophy of Nietzsche*, in *Nietzsche: Philosopher, Psychologist, Antichrist*, ed. W. Kaufmann, Princeton University Press, 1974, p. 508.
33. See Freud's analysis of his own specimen dream in *The Interpretation of Dreams*, 1900, Penguin edition, 1976.
34. See C. G. Jung, *Memories, Dreams, Reflections*, Routledge and Kegan Paul, 1963.
35. Some Jewish theologians have suggested that the Holocaust occurred during an absence or madness of God. See George Steiner, *Language and Silence: Essays 1958–1966*, Peregrine edition, 1979, Postscript, pp.191–205.
36. Elie Wiesel, *Night*, Penguin edition, 1981, p.77.
37. George Steiner, op. cit., p.41.
38. Sylvia Plath, stanzas 3 and 4 from 'The Moon and the Yew Tree', in *Collected Poems*, Faber, 1981, p.173.
39. See, for example, the address given by Chung Hyung-Kyung, Worldwide Anglican Encounter, April 1992.
40. For example, in his forthright poem 'A Stick of Incense', in *Collected Poems*, Macmillan edition, 1979, p. 383.
41. Ursula King, 'Women's Contribution to Contemporary Spirituality' in *Teaching Spirituality, The Way* supplement, Autumn 1994/5, p.32.
42. Wallace Stevens, from 'The Owl in the Sarcophagus', in *Collected Poems*, Knopf, 1981, p.431.
43. Iris Murdoch, *Metaphysics as a Guide to Morals*, Chatto and Windus, 1992, pp.511–12.
44. Clifford Longley in the *Telegraph*, 14 June 1996.
45. David Jones, 'A, a, a, Domine Deus', op. cit.
46. Lesslie Newbigin, *Proper Confidence*, SPCK, 1995, p.94.

Conclusion

A reply to Mrs V. Angry from the Mission Theological Advisory Group

Dear Mrs Angry,

We hope that you have had a chance to look through the material in our book and to see that we do feel challenged by what you and others like you have to say to us. Sometimes the kind of points you raise make us feel very uncomfortable, but also make us feel that we have a great deal to offer to people who are prepared to be open and honest with us about how they see us.

In our book we have tried to listen to what people who are searching for faith have to say about their search and about the nature of their faith. For us, as Christians, we have to find ways of reaching out which do not compromise the integrity of that search and do not seek actively to override people's faith with our own convictions. We entirely agree with you that you are right to see your friend and neighbour Val as a missionary. Yet you should be assured that we are committed to both a view of God and an experience of God which are treasured by us and which we regard as the stuff of our religious commitment and expression.

We are aware that some Christians may think that because we have not given the Christian answers straightaway, we have risked selling the historic faith short, but we do not believe this. In order to witness our faith to people like you, Christians may have to weigh the integrity of their faith against standing alongside you and your anger. We have seen for ourselves that taking risks for the gospel can look like compromise, but we believe exploration of the issues helps us to see the challenges and allows us to make proper response.

We hope that your challenge to us, on the one hand, and our fellow Christians' concerns, on the other, will be met by reconsidering the issues through using the 'things to do'. We would like you really to think about the difficult issues, not in order to give concrete answers, but to raise questions that may help all of us confront more clearly the task of being the Christian Church in the twenty-first century. This is something which all of us in the group, who come from different churches and backgrounds, have been working together to produce: what we *can* do ecumenically to build bridges between the search for faith and the witness of the Church.

Yours sincerely,

Anne Richards

on behalf of the Mission Theological Advisory Group

Glossary of theological terms

Eschaton: We use this term to describe an ultimate act of God, in which there will be established a new creation. The eschatological reality, visionary glimpses of which we obtain from the Book of Revelation, will, we believe, be a total theophany: everything and everyone will express God and praise God. Mission theology therefore also includes eschatological thinking, since our faith in acting in mission is that the loving God has in mind at all times our ultimate destiny.

Evangelism/evangelisation: Evangelism embraces the many ways of reaching out to other people to share the story of what God has done in Jesus Christ. Evangelisation is a slightly broader term. Evangelism is included in mission, but is not synonymous with it. Aggressive acts of evangelism, which put people off, could be said to act against mission. Evangelism needs to be supported by other ways of acting in mission, such as prayer.

Kingdom: A term used by Jesus. Christians speak of the kingdom as a vision of a world order in which God's values are paramount. The kingdom can be spoken of as established now, since Jesus has changed the world for ever, but also as something to be achieved. The latter idea is important for mission theology because it means that we have to look forward to what God intends for us and work towards it through mission, by doing God's will.

Koinonia: This term refers to the bond between Christians, which is also called fellowship. This is fostered by corporate worship. Christians are often described as being in communion with one another, particularly through eucharistic fellowship. When we act in mission, we aim to extend our *koinonia* to others in whatever way we can.

Metanoia: Conversion, a turning round, or radical change. When we act in mission, we open up possibilities for change in people's lives at all levels. While conversion often means the act of making a decision for Christ, it can also refer to the opening up of occasions for repentance and forgiveness, and to the radical action of the Holy Spirit in people's lives.

Missio Dei: This means 'the mission of God'. Mission is seen as an attribute of God. The *missio dei* is commonly understood as the mission of God's love to the world, since God sends his love into the world. God's supreme act of sending love was to send his Son, Jesus Christ, into the world.

Mission of the Church: The Church is an instrument of God's love to the world. The Church exists to serve the mission of God. When Christians act in mission as part of the Church, they participate in the movement of God's love towards all people.

Mission theology: A way of relating what we know about God, Jesus and the Holy Spirit and about the life of the Church, to what we can discover about the *missio dei*. Mission theology also tries to describe what we can do to further the mission of God.

Witness: An act of proclamation, or other ways of showing forth the Good News contained in the gospels. The idea of witness brings out the importance of showing God's love by example.

Index

abortion, and genetic testing 140–41
Alister Hardy Research Centre 47, 75, 100
Allison, C. FitzSimons, *The Cruelty of Heresy* 155
alternative medicine 82
ancestor worship 53–4
angels 60, 98–9
Anselm of Canterbury, St 89, 158, 159
'anthropic principle' of the universe 126, 128, 143
Aquinas, St Thomas 159
Argument from Design 132, 135
Arius 156
aromatherapy 80–82
astrology 85
Athanasius 155
Atkins, Peter 117
Atkinson, Ven. David 175
Attenborough, David 132
Augustine of Canterbury, St 95
autistic people 21

Badham, Paul 157
Bailey, Edward 53, 56
baptism 4, 8-9, 16–17, 36–7
 and implicit religion 46, 50-51, 54, 55
 and individualisation 20
Barley, Nigel 59
Basic Christian Communities 25
Basil of Caesarea 156
being, and being-in-relation 156
belief
 and belonging 3–42, 46–7
 and contemporary spirituality 75–8
 levels of religious belief 2–3, 46–7
 superstitions 45, 58–60, 67, 70, 160
belonging 1, 2
 and belief 3–42, 46–7
 and the Body of Christ 32–3
 and Christian initiation 7–9
 in contemporary society 26–32
 formal and informal 7–8
 scriptural models of 15–18
 to the Church of England 31–2
 to closed societies 29–31
 to a community 25–6
 to the family 22–5
 to me 18–19

in work environments 31
Berkeley, Bishop George 166–7
Bernard of Clairvaux 159
Big Bang 114, 123–4, 125, 127, 133
birth 4-5, 50, 54, 55
 see also baptism
Body of Christ 1–2, 20, 33–5, 37, 94, 153
Body Shop 31
body-centred therapies 74, 80
Bosch, David 164, 166
Bosch, Hieronymus 162
boundaries, and community 29–31, 33–4
brokenness of the world 100
Bunting, Madeleine 49, 50
Byrne, Sr Lavinia 31

Calvin, John 164
Celtic spirituality 74, 91–2, 102
Challen, Canon Peter 24
chaos and complexity theory 128, 145
Chaucer, Geoffrey 161
Christ the Healer 119–20
Christian Initiation and Church Membership 7
Christian unity 33, 164–5
Christmas 58
Church of England
 baptism 9
 belonging to the 31–2
 Doctrine Commission, *The Mystery of Salvation* 46
 and marriage 10, 12
Church of Scotland, and marriage 11
Churches Together 33
churchgoing
 and implicit religion 63
 and religious belief 3–4, 6–7, 11, 46
churchyards *see* graveyards
civic religion 45, 46, 48, 55, 58, 68
collective unconscious 170
Columba, St 95, 96, 98–9
communities
 belonging to a community 25–6
 and boundaries 29–31, 34
 moral 34–5
 religious 30–31
community 1
computer technology 138–9, 143

189

Index

control, being in 78–9, 93–4, 101
conversion, and contemporary spirituality 99–100
Councils of the Church 113, 156
covenant relationship with God 2, 15–17
Cow and Calf 150
creation
  and evolution 131–9
  and implicit religion 61–2
  and science 117, 123–30
creation spirituality 90–93, 101, 102
creed, the 113, 142
Crick, Francis 137

Dante 162
Darwin, Charles 131–2, 133
Darwinism 168
Davie, Grace 4, 32
Davies, Paul 118
Dawkins, Richard 132-3, 134–6, 137
death
  and evolutionary biology 138
  and implicit religion 52–4, 55, 63
  and medical technology 141–2
demonisation 60, 67
Descartes, René 166, 171
disasters, flowers laid at scenes of 56, 57
disciples, fellowship with Jesus 17–18
Docetism 155, 157
Douglas, Mary 48–9
Drabble, Margaret, *The Millstone* 4–5
Drane, John 57–8
Dun I (Iona) 97–8
Dunblane massacre 4, 46, 56–8, 60

Ebionism 155
ecology 87
Einstein's theory of general relativity 122, 169
Eliade, Mircea, *Images and Symbols* 50–51
Eliot, T.S. 119–20, 170, 175
Enlightenment 166–9, 179
Enuma Elish 61
Erasmus 163
eschaton 138, 153
ethics, and technology 139–42, 143
evil
  awareness of 100, 101
  and New Age beliefs 94
  ritual as protection from 54
evolution 111, 131–9, 143

Exclusive Brethren 29
existentialism 173, 174

faith, profession of 8, 11, 36
Falklands War 55
family, belonging to the 22–5
feeling good 79–84, 93–4, 99
fellowship *see koinonia* (fellowship)
feminist theology 172–3
Finney, John 11, 26
folk religion 45, 47–8
  see also implicit religion
formal religion 48, 61–5
fortune-telling 85
Fox, Matthew 90, 91, 95
Frazer, J.G. 49–50
Freeman, Anthony 129
Freud, Sigmund 170
funerals 46, 65
  see also death
future, hope in the 84–7, 94, 115

Gaudium et Spes 92–3, 93–4, 95
Geertz, Clifford 48
gender, and family relationships 23
genetic testing 140–41
Gill, Robin 4, 6–7
Gnosticism 157
God, ontological proof of the existence of 158–9, 178
'God-in-the-gaps' theology 124, 143
good
  feeling good 79–84, 94, 99
  principle of the Good 174
graveyards 52-3
  Reilig Oran (Iona) 98–9
Greenaway, Peter 151
Gregory of Nazianus 156
Gregory of Nyssa 156

Habgood, Dr John 77
Hamilton, Thomas 60
Hampson, Daphne 172
Handley, Paul 4
hands, laying on of 51–2, 62, 83
Harvest festivals 58
Hawking, Stephen 114, 116, 124
healing services 83
Heimbrock, Hans-Gunther 48–9
Heisenberg's Uncertainty Principle 130
hell 46

heresy 154–8, 178
Herschel, Abraham Joshua 62
Hildegard of Bingen 116
Hillborough disaster 4, 46, 56
Hirst, Damien 150, 151
Holocaust 170–71
Hope, Susan 13
Hopkins, Gerard Manley 104
hospice movement 121
Hume, David 167
Huxley, Aldous 84

implicit religion 45–71
 and formal Christianity 61–5
 Network for the Study of 65
 and rituals 45, 48-60
In Memorium notices 54
Independent Churches 65
individualisation 19–21, 26–7, 113
 and contemporary spirituality 76–7
 and the family 25
Industrial Revolution 168
inner city churches 25, 32
Iona pilgrimage 96–7
IVF (in vitro fertilisation) 140–41

Jennings, Elizabeth 126–7
Jesus
 as Christ the Healer 119–20
 fellowship with the disciples 17–18
 resurrection of 155
 and Trinitarianism 156
Jones, David 51, 150
Julian of Norwich, Mother 89, 90
Jung, Carl Gustav 170, 175

Kant, Immanuel 167
Keshishian, Aram 34–5
King, Ursula 173
koinonia (fellowship) 2, 35–6, 156
 and the Body of Christ 32–5

Larkin, Philip 53
Leibniz, Gottfried 166
Leonardo da Vinci 162–3
liberation theologies 154
life sciences 111, 131–9
Locke, John 166
Loyola, Ignatius 164
Luther, Martin 164

McFadyen, Alistair 20
MacIntyre, Alasdair 152
marriage 9–12
 and implicit religion 46, 51, 54, 55, 59, 65
Marvell, Andrew 87
Marxism 168
May rituals 49–50
medical science 119–21
 alternative medicine 82
 and ethics 139–42, 143
 medieval worldview 160–62
metanoia 99
miracles 116–17
Montefiore, Bishop Hugh 117–18
moral communities 34–5
Morris, Colin 6
Morris, Desmond 132
motherhood of God 88–9
Murdoch, Iris 174
music, and contemporary spirituality 94–5
Mystic Meg 85

Nasimiyu-Wasike, Anne 119
National Socialism 62
natural world, and contemporary spirituality 87–94
Negro spirituals 64
Network for the Study of Implicit Religion 65
networks, and participation 26–7
New Age practices 3, 19, 22, 74, 87, 94, 99
 and conversion 99
 and the future 85–6
 therapies 80–82
new religious movements (NRM) 3, 19–20, 23–4, 27, 29–30, 31
Newbigin, Bishop Lesslie 166, 167–8, 176–7, 179
Newell, J. Philip 96–9
Newman, John Henry 62–3
Nicea, Council of 156
Nietzsche, Friedrich 168–9, 171

ontological proof, of the existence of God 158–9, 178–9

Paley, William 133
Palmer, Martin 89–90, 92
Pärt, Arvo 95
Pearl (poem) 162
pharmakon 119–20

Index

pick'n'mix society 22, 74, 83, 175
Pink Floyd 86
Plath, Sylvia 172
post-materialism 21–2, 36, 77–8, 79
post-modernism 77, 86, 150–52, 153, 176, 178, 179
  and fragmentation 35
Potter, Dennis 140
power
  and being in control 78–9
  and implicit religion 63–4
profession of faith 8, 11
Protestantism 164
pubgoing, ritual of 56
public truth, religion as 167–8
PVS (Persistent Vegetative State) 141

Raine, Craig 116
RCIA (Rite of Christian Initiation of Adults) 11
Reformation 163–5
religious communities 30–31
religious education 116
Remembrance Sunday 54, 55, 57, 66
Renaissance 162–3
renewal, and contemporary spirituality 94–9
rituals, and implicit religion 45, 48–60, 64–5, 66, 67
Robinson, Martin 23
Roddick, Anita 31
Roman Catholic Church 9, 11, 31–2
Runcie, Archbishop Robert 142

Sabellian believers 157
Sacks, Oliver 18, 21, 116
Sagan, Carl 138
St Marylebone Centre for Healing and Counselling 32, 82, 83
Salam, Abdus 117
scepticism 165
science 110–46
  choices between religion and 117–18
  complementarity of Christianity and 118–23, 142
  consequences of scientific advances 114–17
  evolutionary theories 131–9, 143
  and the media 114
  medical 119–21, 139–42, 144
  teaching in schools 115–16
  technology and ethics 140–42

Scott, James C. 63–4
Sea of Faith movement 129, 169
self-realisation 79, 99
self-worth 74, 78–9, 80
sexual abuse, Christian survivors of 60
Sheppard, Bishop David 56
sick people, laying of hands on 51–2
Society of Jesus 164
solitary confinement 20
Spencer, Stanley 20
Spinoza, Baruch 166
Steiner, George 171
stress management 81–2
Strong AI (Artificial Intelligence) 139
suicide, choice for 173–4
superstition 45, 58–60, 63, 67, 70
  in the medieval worldview 160
Swinburne, Richard 133

Tavener, John 94
technology, and ethics 139–42
therapies, New Age 80–82
Third World 65, 154
Tippett, Michael 121
Trinity 2, 156, 157
  and individualisation 21
Turin Shroud 116

Uncertainty Principle 130
universe
  'anthropic principle' of the 126, 128, 143
  origins of the 123–9
Vaughan, Henry 165
Watson, Lyall 137
Wessels, Anton 62
Weyer, Robert van der 158
Whitman, Walt 128–9
whole person medicine 119–21
Wiesel, Elie 171
Willshaw, Mervyn 120
Wink, Walter 99, 135
Wittgenstein, Ludwig 171
women 23, 172–3
Woodcock, Jeremy 119–20
work environments, believing and belonging in 31
Worlock, Archbishop Derek 56

Yeats, W.B. 79, 173

Zohar, Dahah 127